...ng in all creation will ever be able to separate us from the love of God...

WALK

spiritual insight
from your
favorite musicians

MARK MORING
General Editor

campus life

thirsty(?)™ an imprint of
tyndale house
publishers

Visit Tyndale's exciting Web site at www.tyndale.com

General Editor, Mark Moring
Edited by Lisa A. Jackson
Designed by Jacqueline Noe

Library of Congress Cataloging-in-Publication Data
Walk: spiritual insight from your favorite musicians / Mark Moring, general editor
   p.cm.
  Includes index.
  ISBN 0-8423-6069-7
   1. Teenage girls—Prayer-books and devotions—English. 2. Christian teenagers—Prayer-books and devotions—English. 3. Contemporary Christian musicians—Religious life. 4. Women musicians—Religious life. I. Moring, Mark.
  BV4860 .W337 2003
  248.8'33—dc.21   2002012584

Printed in China
08 07 06 05 04 03
8   7   6   5   4   3   2   1

CONTENTS

CONTENTS CONTINUED

ACKNOWLEDGMENTS

I'd like to thank my colleagues at *Campus Life* magazine for their hard work in helping to put this book together—Krishana Kraft, Chris Lutes, and Amber Penney.

I'd also like to thank the musicians represented in this book for their willingness to share their personal stories—and for their love for the many girls who will read this book. I'd like to thank the musicians' publicists and managers for helping to make this happen—you know who you are!

I'd like to thank my family—Nina, Peter, and Paul—for their love and support for the work that I do. I love you guys!

Finally, I'd like to thank God—the source of all creativity, the giver of life, and the wellspring of an endless grace that never ceases to amaze me.

Mark Moring
GENERAL EDITOR

Introduction

Don't let the CD sales and the music videos and the stage lights fool you. Even though she's one of the most popular singers in Christian music history, Rebecca St. James is sometimes . . . lonely.

She's not the only Christian musician who faces the same types of struggles that you face. Jennifer Knapp struggles with selfishness. Jaci Velasquez struggles with materialism. The three sisters in Out of Eden used to fight all the time—and sometimes they still have arguments. Superchic[k]'s Tricia Brock worries not only about her looks but also about what it really means to be popular.

Yes, you can identify with them. And they can identify with you, too, because they've been there. And they've learned some valuable lessons along the way. That's why they want to share their stories with you—stories you can relate to and learn from as well.

We interviewed more than thirty Christian musicians for this book. From their real-life stories, we've put together a book of devotionals to help you sort out the things you're dealing with—and bring you closer to God.

This book is full of stories relevant to your life. It's also packed with daily Scripture readings and practical suggestions for putting your faith into action right where you are, right now.

So turn the pages, meet some people a lot like you, and begin a journey toward a deeper, more intimate relationship with God.

The Editors of Campus Life

ℱEELING ℒONELY?

ReBecca ST. JaMes

WHEN I FIRST CAME TO the United States from Australia as a young teen, I had to build all new friendships. That was really hard for me—especially since I was homeschooled and not meeting many new people. Sometimes I came home from youth group crying. My parents reminded me that in order to have friends, I had to be a friend. I needed to get out of my comfort zone, reach out, and not just expect people to reach out to me.

We all get lonely sometimes, but God can use those times in a couple of ways. First, we can do what Jesus did when he felt alone: We can grow closer to God. Jesus often went off by himself to be alone with his Father in prayer (Luke 5:16). When we're alone with God, without the distractions of the world, we can hear his voice more clearly.

> God has said, "I will never fail you. I will never forsake you."
>
> HEBREWS 13:5

Second, we can use our lonely times to look at the gifts God has given us. The apostle Peter challenges us: "Each one should use whatever gift he has received to serve others, faithfully administering God's grace in its various forms. If anyone speaks, he should do it as one speaking the very words of God. If anyone serves, he should do it with the strength God provides, so that in all things God may be praised through Jesus Christ" (1 Peter 4:10).

Even when we're lonely, God calls us to serve others. Every day we see people who are hurting and lonely and need a dose of God's great love. Can you imagine what would happen if each one of us, as Christians, took that responsibility to love seriously? Revival would break out! There are people in your life—at school, in your neighborhood—people who would love to know someone cares about them.

The next time you feel lonely, think about the people you could minister to. Think about ways you could serve them in God's name. When you reach out to other people, you're giving them encouragement and God is pleased. That's when you find true joy in life.

THINK ABOUT IT

When Rebecca came home from youth group in tears because she felt friendless, her parents gave her some wise advice: Instead of dwelling on her loneliness, they encouraged Rebecca to concentrate on loving others. That's often the most difficult step to take when we're lonely—to take our eyes off ourselves and turn them to others. Could God be calling you to do something like that today?

SO, WHAT NEXT?

There's something in all of us that just loves a pity party. When we're lonely, there's something oddly satisfying about wallowing in that solitude. We want others to feel sorry for us, too. But how do we rise above that, get beyond ourselves, and think about others?

1. Read Psalm 37:23-28. What does this passage tell you about God's promises to you when you're lonely? Reread verse 26. What does this tell you about steps you can take to get beyond loneliness?

2. If you're lonely, think of one small thing you could do for someone else today, and then try to do it. If you know someone who's lonely, do something kind for him or her today.

3. Consider God's promise that he will never leave you or forsake you. Ask him to make that truth come alive in your heart, and ask him to help you share that same truth with someone else.

Rebecca St. James

3

SHelley BrEen
of Point of Grace

And let us run
with endurance
the race that
God has set
before us.

HEBREWS 12:1

Am I Good at Anything?

I WAS ON THE SOCCER TEAM in sixth grade, but I didn't play very much because I wasn't any good at it.

I tried other sports, without much success. I just wasn't very coordinated. I tried typing class, and I was terrible at it. I tried piano, and I wasn't very good at that either.

It got to the point where I felt like I'd never be good at anything. I made good grades, but I didn't have any hobby or skill where I could say, "I'm decent at that."

At church, people always said, "You need to use your gifts and talents." But I didn't feel like I had any!

Still, I kept trying, even when I wasn't good at something. Even when I hated it, I kept at it. Like piano lessons. I hated practice. It just never clicked for me. But I refused to quit.

Finally, in junior high, I took girls' choir and really enjoyed it. One day at practice, my choir director was teaching me a part when she stopped me and said, "You know what? You're doing really well. You can really sing!"

I was like, "Really?"

A few weeks later, she asked me to sing a solo at our spring concert. I started to wonder, *Could this be the thing for me? Because I've failed at quite a few things . . .*

I kept at it, and I started trying other things—like my church choir, trying out for solos. I wasn't always comfortable doing those things, but I knew I had to at least try.

I never thought that someday I might become a professional singer, but I did know I'd found something I really loved. I'd discovered that I did have a talent after all!

But I never would have found that talent if I weren't so persistent. If I hadn't kept walking through doors that were a little uncomfortable, trying things that made me nervous, I might never have found my gift at all.

THINK ABOUT IT

No matter how many times she failed, Shelley kept getting up and trying again . . . and again and again. Her determination paid off in a big way—she discovered the talent that would eventually lead to a career as a singer. But persistence doesn't always bring great results. Sometimes it brings yet another failure. Still, it's often persistence itself that helps us grow, whether we can see tangible results or not.

SO, WHaT NEXT?

Shelley said, "Even when I hated it, I kept at it." That's a great working definition of persistence. What is it that you don't like to do, but should keep trying anyway?

1. Read Romans 5:3-5. Why should we "rejoice . . . when we run into problems and trials"? How can problems possibly be "good for us"? How do such times show us "how dearly God loves us"? Think of a time when you persevered through something difficult. How did it help you grow in your faith?

2. Memorize Philippians 4:13. Put the verse on an index card, and place it where you'll need regular encouragement to persist in a task. If it's piano lessons, tape it to the piano. If it's your early-morning run, write "Philippians 4:13" on your shoes so you can look down and see it as a reminder. You get the idea.

3. Ask God to help you "run with endurance the race" he has given you—even the parts that aren't much fun.

Shelley Breen
OF POINT OF GRACE

WE WERE ALWAYS FIGHTING!

Photo by Robert Ascroft

ANDREA BACA
OF OUT OF EDEN

Pride leads to arguments; those who take advice are wise.

PROVERBS 13:10

MY SISTERS AND I have often fought, but it was at its worst on our first concert tour. Three teenage sisters, stuck together in a van for three months. And even though a chaplain traveled with us to help us stay in line, our mom, who usually broke up our fights, wasn't with us.

It was a recipe for disaster. Usually, we fought over something stupid, like what somebody was wearing or who we were hanging out with. Or we'd just start talking about politics, and then it would get ugly and turn into this huge deal.

The chaplain who toured with us was not only supposed to keep us grounded in our faith but also to hold us accountable for our behavior. And he had his hands full with us. He could see it all over us: strife, bickering, all kinds of ugly stuff. One day he literally had to break us up because we were in each other's faces, screaming.

He said, "You know, before you're sisters in blood, you're sisters in Christ. And you must treat each other that way. Would you say 'I hate you' to your sister in Christ?"

We said no.

He said, "Then you shouldn't do that to each other." That's all he said. But it was enough. And those words have always stuck with me.

Sure, we still fight sometimes, but not nearly as often. And we've all learned how to say, "I'm sorry."

When we were younger, we never felt like we had to apologize to each other. But when you don't apologize, you can harbor bitterness, even without realizing it. Then all of a sudden, you realize you don't like this person because of all the things he or she has done.

So now we always apologize if we've had a fight. That way, nobody holds grudges. Nobody keeps score. The slate is wiped clean every time.

That's the way it should be between sisters in Christ.

SO, WHaT NEXT?

Andrea says she and her sisters usually fought over "something stupid," and that's often the way it is. But the girls were also wise enough to listen to some good advice and take it to heart. What about you?

1. Read today's verse (Proverbs 13:10). What does it mean that "pride leads to arguments"? This thirteenth chapter of Proverbs is full of great advice for handling conflicts. Read verses 1-3, 10, 13, 16, and 18. What do these verses tell you about how you can better relate to your own siblings?

2. Make a list of all the things that annoy you about a sibling. Then tear it up, saying the words, "I forgive you." Now list all the things that you appreciate about that sibling, including special memories. Then write a nice note to your sibling, including some of the things on your "good" list.

3. Read Proverbs 11:29-30. Ask God to help you be "life-giving fruit" to your siblings.

It's not unusual for siblings to argue and get into occasional fights. But if the bickering becomes constant or the quarrels too intense, the relationship can be severely damaged. That's why it's important to keep the conflict to a minimum—and to have the courage to apologize afterward. It's also important to remember, as Andrea and her sisters learned, that your siblings are your brothers and sisters in Christ. How does that affect your relationship with each other?

Andrea Baca
OF OUT OF EDEN

Photo by Christian Lantry

StAcie ORrico

I'll Be There for You

SONYA AND I have been best friends since fourth grade. We've been pretty much inseparable since then, at each other's house every day, sharing all kinds of inside jokes and lots of laughs.

We knew each other so well. Or so I thought.

When we were both fourteen, I learned Sonya was suffering from anorexia nervosa, an eating disorder. Along with losing weight, she struggled a lot emotionally.

Share each other's troubles and problems, and in this way obey the law of Christ.

GALATIANS 6:2

I didn't know what to do, except to continue being her friend, loving her, and encouraging her. I wrote a song called "Dear Friend," where I tell Sonya, "I feel so helpless. I see you sit in silence. As you face new pain each day, I feel there's nothing I can do. I know you don't feel pretty, even though you are."

And that's true. Sonya is a beautiful girl who was never overweight at all. I just wish she had known how much God values her before she went down this road. There's a verse that says God rejoices over us with singing (Zephaniah 3:17). That's what he does for Sonya. I just want Sonya to understand that her worth has nothing to do with the way she looks.

I've tried to show her how valuable she is just by being with her. Sometimes Sonya just needed someone to come and share a meal with her, to just have fun and make it not seem like her whole life revolved around the sandwich she was supposed to eat at lunch. She just needed somebody to listen to her and encourage her when she was going through a hard time.

I wanted to be that for her. It was never like, "Oh, this is getting hard, so I don't want to be friends anymore." It was like, "You've been there for me through my hard times, and I will always be there for you. There's no question about it. You're my best friend."

And she still is.

That's what God does for us. It's the least I could do for Sonya.

THINK ABOUT IT

How do you respond to friends who are hurting? Do you ignore them because you don't know what to say? Or do you reach out to them and show them love? Caring for friends who are going through some kind of struggle can sometimes feel intimidating, especially if it's a struggle you've never experienced. But your friends need to know you're there for them. What are some ways you can show that?

SO, WHaT NEXT?

When things got hard for Sonya, Stacie didn't give up on her. Instead, Stacie looked for ways to help. That probably wasn't always fun for Stacie, especially when Sonya was down. But sometimes helping a friend means making a sacrifice.

1. Read Mark 2:1-12. How did the four men show love for their paralyzed friend? What are some ways you can carry a hurting friend to Jesus?

2. Even a phone call can make a difference to someone who's hurting. Do you have any friends who might need to hear from you this week? Don't put it off. Let them know you're willing to listen if they want to talk. Or invite them to a movie. Your friends may find a lot of comfort in not having to say anything at all.

3. Another great way to carry your friends' burdens is to pray for them. Ask God to meet their needs and to show you how to be an encouragement.

Stacie Orrico

Photo by Ben Pearson

JeNNifer KnaPp

THEY PICKED ME UP

WHEN I GRADUATED from high school and headed off to college, I was still trying to figure out a lot of stuff about life. But I was sure of this:

God did not exist. And nothing would change my mind. I had a foul mouth. I was into drinking and sex.

And I didn't like Christians. That is, until I met a few—starting with Ami, my roommate.

Sometimes Ami talked about her faith. But mostly, she just lived in such a way that I could tell there was something different about her.

I rarely felt judged by Ami. Rather than saying, "Wow, aren't you a mess?" she showed me compassion.

For example, one night I stumbled into my dorm really drunk and nauseated. I'm sure I was quite a sight. But Ami was gracious. She helped me into the bathroom and held back my hair while I threw up. Then she helped me into bed.

The next morning, I was miserable. Ami said, "I don't think you're miserable because of a hangover. I think you're miserable because you're hurting inside." She said it with grace. And she was right.

And then there was Paula. She never judged me either. She gave me Bible verses in an envelope every day. She'd say, "If you want to read these, just open the envelope."

I started reading them. I started asking questions. Ami and

> If one person falls, the other can reach out and help. But people who are alone when they fall are in real trouble.
>
> ECCLESIASTES 4:10

Paula listened and answered and loved me, even though I kept saying, "I'm an atheist. This isn't real."

But it was real. For three months, Ami, Paula, and others—many of whom were praying for me all along—lovingly proved it to me in so many ways. And their love pointed me to God. That October, my freshman year in college, I joined them. I became a Christian too.

Thanks to Ami and Paula, my journey had begun. And thanks to God, I started growing.

Still am.

SO, WHAT NEXT?

It's easy to love our Christian friends. And it's pretty easy to care for the "nice" non-Christians in our world. But it's a lot harder to love people who not only live lousy lifestyles but are also downright hostile to what we believe. How do we show love to those people?

1. Read Luke 10:25-37. Samaritans were a racial minority despised by Israelites. What does this passage tell you about loving someone you wouldn't normally love? How is the message of this passage similar to today's verse, Ecclesiastes 4:10?

2. Think of someone who's "fallen" and may need your help to get up. List five things that person probably needs. Circle one need you can meet this week and do whatever it takes to meet it.

3. Ask God to give you the compassion and mercy the Samaritan man showed in Luke 10. Ask him to give you the boldness to put that kindness into action. You may be showing someone Jesus!

Jennifer Knapp

Photo by Melinda DiMauro

I FELT SO UGLY

Tricia Brock
OF SUPERCHIC[K]

ZITS AREN'T GREAT
for your self-esteem. I
ought to know, because I
struggled with acne all
through high school.

Some days I would
look in the mirror and
just feel so ugly. And then
when I'd get to school, it
seemed like everyone was
staring at me. That made
me feel even uglier.

Everybody struggles
with something. I never
worried much about my
weight, but I know it can

Charm is
deceptive, and
beauty does
not last;
but a woman
who fears the
Lord will be
greatly
praised.

PROVERBS 31:30

be a big struggle for girls who never feel like they're thin
enough. For others, it might be something else. For me, it was
acne, and it took me a while to get over being so self-conscious
about it.

These days, I often meet girls at our concerts who are
struggling with something. At one recent show, I talked about
my struggles with acne. Afterward, this girl came up to me and
said, "I struggle with acne too. I know it seems like a small
thing, but honestly, it's one of the hardest things to deal with.
I feel ugly."

I can totally relate to what she said. But the only way we
can break free of our insecurities is not to worry about what
other people think and to remember that when God looks at
us, he loves us just as we are—just the way he created us.

That's why I really like the song "Let It Be" on our first
CD. The words apply to me so well:

We could believe in ourselves more, we could try for unique

Instead of trying to conform, we could defy what they tell us

Don't buy the lies they sell us . . .

Let it go, let it be, brick by brick we can be free

Let it go, let it be, brick by brick we can believe

in the person God intended us to be

That's my theme song, and I plan on singing it—and believing it and living it—for the rest of my life.

SO, WHAT NEXT?

Imagine yourself sixty years from now. Your looks will definitely have changed—those facial blemishes will have changed to wrinkles and your hair color to gray. So, when your looks have faded, what will you have left?

1. Read today's verse (Proverbs 31:30). What does this verse say about charm and beauty? What's more important than beauty? What does it mean to "fear the Lord"? And how will doing that affect the way we look at ourselves?

2. Talk with an elderly Christian woman about what part of her appearance she struggled with as a teenager. Ask how her perspective on appearance has changed over the years and what caused her change in perspective.

3. Thank God for how he created you. Ask him to help you focus more on fearing and loving him than worrying about the parts of your appearance you wish you could change.

Tricia says she struggled with acne during high school. How do you struggle with the way you look? Even if Tricia's face had been acne-free, she probably would have found something else she didn't like about herself. It seems there's always something about our outward appearance we desire to change. If it's not our face, it's our hair, figure, or even height. How can we be content with the person God has made us to be?

Tricia Brock

OF SUPERCHIC[K]

JAci VelaSquez

In Search of True Love

SOMETIMES IT SEEMS like everyone I know is searching for true love. I admit I wouldn't mind finding it myself. It feels great to have someone pay attention to you, care about you, and hold you tenderly. But love and romance can fool us sometimes. They can lead us into thinking things about ourselves that just aren't true.

One of my friends has a deep need for attention from the opposite sex. She's a great and beautiful person, but if she doesn't have a boyfriend, she feels ugly and worthless.

But boyfriends are just people. They'll make mistakes; they'll let you down. They won't always be sensitive. So as long as my friend looks to her boyfriend for happiness, she'll be disappointed. But I really can't be too hard on her, because there are times I've wanted romantic love to fulfill all my needs and make me feel special too. But should I expect so much of another human being?

It's taken me a long time to realize God's love is the only kind of love that will never disappoint me. God's love, and God's love alone, allows me to see my real value, worth, and beauty. And when I learn to love myself as God loves me, I'll be better prepared to love others—including that special guy who will one day come into my life.

It's funny. When you fall in love or have a big crush on somebody, your whole world—everything you think and feel—

> This is real love. It is not that we loved God, but that he loved us and sent his Son as a sacrifice to take away our sins.
>
> 1 JOHN 4:10

I will never forsake you.

revolves around that person. It's a fantastic feeling! But isn't that sort of how you felt when you first met Jesus? He became the love of your soul!

We need to stop and remember that sometimes. And we need to keep our love for God alive by talking to him, turning to him with all of our needs, and showing our love for him by the way we live. When this happens, everything else will fall into place—including our desire for romance.

SO, WHaT NEXT?

As Jaci wrote, if we expect humans to keep our "happiness tank" full at all times, we're surely headed for disappointment. Yes, people can be the source of great joy most of the time. But there's only one source of eternal joy—the only one who will never let us down. How do we love him in return?

1. Read 1 John 4:7-19. Write down three things describing God's love for us. Read verse 10 and ask, "How could God love me even though I didn't love him?" Read verse 18 and ask, "Why do I have fears if God loves me perfectly?"

2. We know what God's love for us looks like: Christ on the cross. What does your love for God look like? List ten ways you can show your love for God, and practice at least one of them today.

3. Thank God for his incredible love. Ask him to show you how to best express your love for him.

THINK ABOUT IT

Have you ever dated a guy—or maybe just had a crush on one—only to be let down? Unless he's the world's biggest creep, some of your disappointment probably came from your own unrealistic expectations. Where'd those expectations come from? Movies? Romance novels? Or your own needs—to be loved, to be rescued, or simply to feel better about yourself? Can any guy on the planet deliver that?

Jaci Velasquez

I WAS CRUSHED

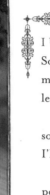

TiNa ATkins
of MARY MARY

I USED TO BE pretty chubby. Sometimes people would tease me about it, but I just had to learn to put up with it.

But one day, somebody said something that cut so deeply, I'll never forget it.

I was hanging out with these popular girls—you know, the kind of girls everybody looks up to because they're funny and they've got all the friends. Somewhere in the conversation, I made fun of this chubby guy who had a crush on me—but I didn't want him to like me because he just annoyed me to death.

Anyway, one of the girls heard what I said, and she was like, "I don't know why you're talking, because you're fat yourself!"

When she said that, I was crushed. She broke me down so bad. That comment stuck with me, and it still does to this day. A hundred years later, I'll still remember that.

I was so self-conscious about my weight problem that I tried to cope with it by being funny. I tried to be extra goofy to make people laugh so they wouldn't focus on my weight. But by doing that, I was programming myself to act a certain way to get people to like me—for the wrong reasons.

Then somebody told me something that really made a difference: "God made you beautiful, and you're good enough because God said so."

I guess I'd always known that, but for some reason, it

You made all the delicate, inner parts of my body and knit me together in my mother's womb. Thank you for making me so wonderfully complex! Your workmanship is marvelous— and how well I know it.

PSALM 139:13-14

started to sink in right then: I'm good enough because God says so.

I realized then that nobody's perfect, not even the people we think have it made. They have insecurities too; they have things they want to fix.

We have to learn to love ourselves the way God made us, and to forget what others say we should look like. I'll never look like a model. I'll never have that perfect look. But I will be me.

And God says that's good enough.

SO, WHaT NEXT?

Have you ever seen anyone knit something? It can take months of hard work just to make one sweater. Today's passage says God himself knit you together—every single cell—with his own hands. That's how much he cares for you.

1. Today's passage comes from a psalm where David marvels not only at how well God knows him but also how God is always with him—no matter where he goes. Read Psalm 139:1-12. How can these words encourage you when you're down?

2. Get five blank note cards. From Psalm 139, write one encouraging truth on each card—like "Everywhere I go, God is with me" or "God made me with his own hands." Seal them in stamped envelopes, address them to yourself, and give them to a friend. Ask the friend to mail them to you at random times over the next few weeks. (Or you can send the notes to a friend who's hurting.)

3. Read the last two verses of Psalm 139, and make these words your prayer to God today.

THINK ABOUT IT

We sometimes like to believe that others' cruel remarks don't hurt our feelings, but they do—just like with Tina, who says she felt like scum after someone said something mean about her weight. Have you ever felt that way? Tina was self-conscious about her weight; what are you self-conscious about? What do you think of Tina's statement, "I'm good enough because God says so"? Does that describe the way you feel about yourself?

Tina Atkins

OF MARY MARY

I BLEW IT!

Photo by Michael Gomez

Paige

WHEN I WAS A FRESHMAN, I made the varsity softball team at my high school, which was a pretty big deal for me. But it was also hard in some ways.

First, since I was the youngest player, I didn't know anyone very well. Second, I was one of the only players who couldn't drive. Finally—and most importantly—it was hard for me to take a stand for my faith, because I really wanted to fit in. I didn't want them to think I was weird.

That year, our team manager was someone you wouldn't necessarily call cool. None of my teammates ever hesitated to remind her of this, either, which made it very difficult for me. I knew I should reach out to this girl or at least refrain from harassing her. But it was hard for me to stand up against my whole team since I was so young.

One time on the bus when everyone was laughing at her, I went along and even added a few clever jokes of my own—just to make myself look good in front of my teammates. Afterward, I was disgusted with myself. I could've stood up for that girl and tried to handle things God's way. But I blew it and went along with the crowd.

Looking back, I wish I would've let God use me to make a difference in that girl's life. There were so many things I could have done right, but didn't—all because I wanted to be accepted by my teammates.

> Don't use foul or abusive language. Let everything you say be good and helpful, so that your words will be an encouragement to those who hear them.
>
> EPHESIANS 4:29

As a result, I've learned it's important to say things that build others up and don't discourage. I still blow it, though. There are times that I think, *Why did I just say that? I didn't need to say that.*

I pray that those times will be few, and that I will please God with my actions and my words. And when I do blow it, I pray I'll have the guts to admit it—and to make things right.

Recall a time when you were in a situation similar to the one Paige describes. Were you the one being made fun of, the one doing the name-calling, or the one who kept silent? If you were the one being ridiculed, how did that make you feel? If you were being mean or silent, how did you feel about it afterward? What should you have done differently?

SO, WHaT NEXT?

The person who came up with the little ditty "words will never hurt me" was obviously never called any names. If you've ever been put down or made fun of, you know how much words can hurt. As Christians, we're called to love others and treat them as we want to be treated, which means being careful with our words.

1. Read Proverbs 16:24. When has someone spoken to you with the kind of words described here? How did they make you feel? Now think about words that are the opposite of what the verse describes. What effect do they have? (See Proverbs 12:18, 15:1, and 18:8 for ideas.)

2. Think of some specific ways to encourage others with your words. (Hint: One idea might be to write a thank-you card to a friend, family member, or even a church leader who has impacted your life.) Then put your ideas into practice.

3. Read Psalm 141:3. Make this your prayer when you're tempted to say things that will tear others down.

Paige

19

Photo by Soren Mork

Cindy MOrgan

*T*HANKS, *M*OM AND *D*AD!

STANDING BACKSTAGE, I felt like I would explode from worry.

I was getting ready to sing in a talent contest at the local mall. I would soon walk onstage before a sea of faces. I was a high school senior, and my music teacher had encouraged me to sing more often in front of audiences. She wanted me to stretch myself by trying new things. But right then, I felt the "stretching" would pull me apart!

I took a deep breath, muttered a quick prayer, and walked onstage. Anxiously, I skimmed the audience and found my smiling parents. I smiled back, and suddenly felt a bit more confident. I started singing my first song, and with each measure, my confidence grew. When the knot in my stomach started coming back, I'd look toward my family for reassuring smiles. They didn't let me down. By the time I started my second song, I was actually having a good time! It was such an incredible feeling.

Several acts came after me, and then came the judging. The announcer read the winners' names, starting with fourth place. By the time he got to the second-place winner, I was discouraged. I thought I'd done well, but apparently not well enough. Then . . .

"First place goes to Cindy Morgan!"

I couldn't believe it. In a very short time, I'd gone from intense jitters to winning! I glanced at my mom and dad. They were cheering wildly. I couldn't stop smiling.

If you honor your father and mother, "you will live a long life, full of blessing."

EPHESIANS 6:3

20

What an encouragement my parents are—not just then, but always. They've always stuck with me, in both good and bad times. They've been by my side even when I haven't been a winner.

That day, I learned an unforgettable lesson about the love of family. Unlike feelings that come and go, the love of those who really care about me is constant and dependable. That gives me a good, lasting feeling and makes me incredibly grateful.

Thanks, Mom and Dad, for being there—no matter what.

SO, WHaT NEXT?

Think about how you've related to your parents the last few days. Were the interactions mostly good? If so, ask God to continue to bless your relationship. If not, ask him to show you ways to patch things up.

1. Today's verse (Ephesians 6:3) is actually one of the Ten Commandments. Read Deuteronomy 5:16, the only commandment that includes a promise of good things if we obey it. Why do you think God included a promise with this commandment? How does that promise help you honor your parents?

2. List ten or twelve good things your parents have done for you—ranging from big things ("they love me") to the mundane ("they changed my diaper when I was a baby"). Now list five good things you can do for them. Do at least one of them in the next twenty-four hours.

3. Thank the Lord for your parents. Ask him to help you honor your mom and dad, and to give you a great relationship with them.

THINK ABOUT IT

While Cindy paints a positive picture of her relationship with her parents, that doesn't mean she didn't sometimes argue with them. Many teenagers, anxious for independence, have disagreements with their parents. Many simply don't think their parents are cool. Maybe that's you, maybe not. In any case, take some time to think about some of the good things your parents have done for you, and ask yourself, "Now, what can I do for them?"

Cindy Morgan

GOD WITH SKIN ON

Photo by Kristin Barlowe

ReBecca ST. JaMes

I was hungry,
and you fed me.
I was thirsty,
and you gave me
a drink. I was a
stranger, and
you invited me
into your home.
I was naked, and
you gave me
clothing.
I was sick, and
you cared for
me. I was in
prison, and you
visited me.

MATTHEW 25:35-36

I GREW UP OUTSIDE SYDNEY, Australia, and have vivid childhood memories of visiting the city—the harbor bridge, the funny-looking opera house, the people, and the huge buildings. It was all very "wow" to me.

But the experiences I remember most are walks downtown with my family when I'd see people begging for money. I felt so sorry for them, especially the people who were disabled or in wheelchairs. I remember thinking it would be so cool if someday I could buy a house in Sydney where poor people could come, have a hot meal, take a warm bath, put on clean clothes, and have a place to stay.

I don't know whether God will lead me to do that in the future—it's all in his hands. But it's so important that I be faithful wherever God has put me to show his love and compassion to everyone—young, old, rich, poor—everyone!

Most of us have so much at our fingertips, so it's hard to imagine really needing anything. But check out these statistics: More than thirty thousand children die every day in the world from illnesses brought on by malnutrition. Ninety percent of these deaths could've been prevented if the children had clean water and sanitation. Every night, one in five children around the world goes to bed hungry.

Reaching out to the poor and the lonely is something God calls all of us to do. One way you can make a difference is to sponsor a child through a relief organization. If you can't afford to do it on your own, sponsor a child with some friends or your youth group. It costs less than a dollar a day, but it makes a big difference to the children you help.

There are many other ways to show God's love and compassion to others—like helping out in the community, mowing a neighbor's lawn for free, doing the dishes at home, or going on a missions trip during a school break. We're really called to be "God with skin on."

THINK ABOUT IT

When was the last time you were really hungry and had nothing to eat? Or needed a warm place to sleep? The statistics Rebecca shared give us a better idea of how some people live, especially children. Many of us have been extremely blessed with necessities like food and shelter, so we have a lot to offer those in need. What do you have to offer—even in your own hometown?

SO, WHaT NEXT?

God calls us to help the needy. What can you do to increase your awareness of the needs around you? How can you turn awareness into action?

1. Read 1 John 3:16-18. What does this passage tell you about love? How does this passage relate to today's verse (Matthew 25:35-36)?

2. Rebecca mentions ways we can show compassion. Make a "to-do" list of ways you can show compassion in your community, like serving at a soup kitchen or helping with a food drive. Then continue the list with ways you can show compassion to those around the world, like sponsoring a child. Finally, make a commitment to put one of those ideas into action soon.

3. Thank God for the blessings you've received. Ask him to make you more aware of those in need and to guide you in turning that awareness into action.

Rebecca St. James

I FELT LIKE A FAILURE

TeRry JOnes
of POINT OF GRACE

I WAS IN SHOW CHOIR in tenth grade, and I just loved it. I knew that was what I wanted to do for the rest of my time in high school, and maybe even in college.

So, when I tried out for show choir my junior year, I was shocked when I didn't make it. All my friends made it, but I didn't.

I was so sad that I cried about it. I just didn't understand why I didn't make it. I felt like a failure.

And I was lonely. Show choir was more than just an opportunity to sing and dance. It was my niche, my way of belonging, the place where I hung out with my best friends. My whole junior year was very difficult, especially when the show choir performed. I'd see my friends onstage, and I'd think about how much I wanted to be with them.

God taught me something about humility during that time. But you know what? As sad as I was, I decided I wasn't going to have a pity party. I decided to do something about it. I thought, *Well, I guess I'll have to try harder, because obviously I wasn't good enough this time. I'll just have to do better next time.*

The main reason I didn't make show choir wasn't because of my voice, but because I was a lousy dancer. You had to dance fairly well to be in show choir.

So I found a dance instructor, and I worked really hard for the whole next year, trying to get to the point where I could actually do some dancing.

[W]henever trouble comes your way, let it be an opportunity for joy. . . . [Y]our endurance has a chance to grow. So let it grow, for when your endurance is fully developed, you will be strong in character and ready for anything.

JAMES 1:2-4

And I kept thinking of James 1:2-4, which tells us that trials will only strengthen us and make us strong in character. I took a lot of strength from that truth and kept on going.

The next year, my senior year, I made it. I was back in show choir!

THINK ABOUT IT

Because of her deep disappointment, Terry could have spent the next year sulking, getting angry, or just giving up on show choir altogether. Instead, she decided to do something productive: She turned her disappointment into action by working with a dance instructor. What about you? What do you do with your disappointments and heartaches? Do they make you a bitter person? Or, in the end, do they make you a better person?

SO, WHaT NEXT?

Are you dealing with disappointment? Is there something in your life that's especially difficult? Are you angry about certain circumstances? How do you go about moving forward?

1. Today's passage (James 1:2-4) is similar to Romans 5:3-5, which teaches us how to deal with hard times. The Romans passage says difficulties are actually "good for us." Do you agree or disagree? Why? Think of some ways that hard times have actually helped you.

2. Write three potential trials you could face—breaking up with a boyfriend, flunking a big test, whatever comes to mind. Now, write something positive you might do to turn a negative event into something that will help develop your character and make you stronger.

3. Reread Romans 5:3-5, saying the words to God as a prayer: "Help me, God, to rejoice when I run into problems and trials, for I know they are good for me. . . ." And so on.

Terry Jones
OF POINT OF GRACE

I'm Saving This Gift!

Photo by Ben Pearson

NaTalie LaRue
of LaRue

AS CHRISTIANS, we sometimes think that just because we're committed to sexual purity until marriage, we're somehow immune to falling in that area. But that's so untrue.

A few years ago, a good friend—a strong Christian—had a steady boyfriend. She never thought they'd have sex. But she came to me one day and said she was pregnant. She was seventeen.

She kept the baby, but her boyfriend didn't stick around. And she had to face some consequences. Some were obvious: She was a full-time single mom, and she had to postpone her college dreams.

Other consequences weren't so visible. She later got engaged to a great guy, and they remained abstinent until their wedding day. But on that day, she felt impure because she was no longer a virgin. She wanted the best for her husband, but she was heartbroken that she couldn't give him something she'd already given to somebody else.

That's something I never want to go through.

The Bible tells us our bodies belong to the Lord, and that we're supposed to honor him with everything we do. That's what I want to do. And that's why I have an accountability partner—my mom. She holds me accountable for everything and asks me the hard questions. When I come home from a date, I know I've got to answer to Mom!

If that's not motivation enough, I also want to avoid the mistake my friend made. I want to be able to bring my future

> God wants you to be holy, so you should keep clear of all sexual sin. Then each of you will control your body and live in holiness and honor.
>
> 1 THESSALONIANS 4:3-4

husband the precious gift of waiting for him my whole life, of waiting until our wedding night. There's no bigger gift I can give him—giving him my whole heart and my whole body and my whole soul, with no regrets whatsoever.

That's a gift God has given me to give to one person, and one person alone—not to pass around. It's a precious gift, and I intend to save it for my wedding day.

SO, WHaT NEXT?

Natalie has talked to many married couples about abstinence. Many of them waited until marriage to have sex, and many did not. Of those who didn't, Natalie says, "Every one of them said they wished they'd waited." Which kind of couple will you and your husband be?

1. Read 1 Thessalonians 4:1-12 so you can get the full context of today's passage. What are some other ways you can live to please God? The beginning of verse 12 gives yet another motivation for living a godly life. What is it?

2. Volunteer at a crisis pregnancy center. While the girls and young women there have made some poor choices, you can offer them a message of grace, forgiveness, and new life (see 1 Corinthians 6:9-11).

3. Ask God to help you remain abstinent until your wedding day. And if you've already had sex, claim the truth of 1 Corinthians 6:11 and thank God for making you pure again.

THINK ABOUT IT

What motivates you to remain sexually pure until your wedding day? Fear of pregnancy or disease? Having to tell your parents? God's commands? These are all strong motivations. But Natalie gives another good reason for waiting: Think of sex as the best gift you could ever give anyone, a precious gift saved exclusively for your future husband, a gift that only you can give him. That's a gift he'll cherish forever.

Natalie La Rue
OF LaRue

*T*HE *C*OLOR OF *L*OVE

Photo by Robert Ascroft

NiCole C. MullEn

When I started dating David, who's now my husband, it really bothered me to hold his hand in public. People would watch us because he's Caucasian and I'm African-American.

But the stares and occasional rude comments didn't bother him. He never thought twice about dating me. The color of my skin just wasn't an issue. I remember he told me that I needed to get over that and stop letting it bother me. Eventually I did. I just needed to be reminded that it didn't matter what people thought. We may have looked very different on the outside, but we had a mutual love for each other.

Today, David and I have two kids—a biological daughter who's biracial and an adopted son who's African-American.

We tell our kids that when God made each person in our family, he knew which color would be best for each one of us. We also tell them love isn't about color. We believe the various colors in our family only help us see how great God's love is for people of all races and backgrounds. That's why, when my daughter was born, I wrote this song "Black, White, Tan." Here are some of the lyrics:

> Mama looks like coffee, Daddy looks like cream
> Baby is a mocha drop, American dream
> All the colors in the rainbow is in her family tree . . .
> And her soul gives a smile
> 'Cause she understands
> That love is black, white, tan . . .

And the most important piece of clothing you must wear is love. Love is what binds us all together in perfect harmony.

COLOSSIANS 3:14

28

Everyone is precious in the Father's sight
It don't matter red or yellow, black or white
He just loves you 'cause He loves you
And I tell you this is true
You are not a color and the color is not you

It's just like the old Sunday school song goes: Jesus loves all the children of the world—and that includes everyone, no matter their age, color, or ethnicity.

Love for God and each other matters most. That's a truth we all can live by.

SO, WHaT NEXT?

In Colossians, Paul talks about the different types of people who made up the church at that time: "Jew, Greek, circumcised, uncircumcised." Even though these people were very diverse, they couldn't let their differences affect their relationships. When it comes to building good friendships, what matters most?

1. Read Colossians 3:11-15. What really matters in life? How should we "clothe" ourselves? Which of these character traits do you need to show more of?

2. Think about somebody in your youth group or school who's another race or from a different culture. What makes this person unique, beyond physical appearance? A talent? A special quality? Write this person a note to share your appreciation of who he or she is.

3. Thank God for the unique way he created you. Confess those times you've criticized your own appearance or judged someone else by their outer appearance. Ask God to make your character, especially your love, your most obvious personal trait—more obvious than your physical appearance.

THINK ABOUT IT

People may have thought Nicole and David should be defined by their different skin tones, but it was their love for God and for each other that really mattered. When we describe people, we usually start with their physical appearance. But we shouldn't end there. Do people use your outward appearance to define who you are? Have you ever judged someone's character by the way they look on the outside? How can we overcome this tendency to judge only from the outside?

Nicole C. Mullen

29

DAniElle YoUng
OF CAEDMON'S CALL

My Body, My Image?

DURING MY FRESHMAN YEAR of high school, I lost a bunch of weight. I wasn't trying to. It just kind of happened.

Pretty soon after that, I started getting a lot of attention, especially from guys. For the first time, they were asking me out.

I immediately noticed the connection between the attention and my weight loss. So in my mind I began to think, *Skinny = People liking me.* And that became a big-time obsession for me.

Every time I would eat even one bite of anything I thought was fattening, I would think, *Okay, what can I do to work this off? I've got to exercise. And I can't have any fat tomorrow.*

I thought about my weight so much that it completely consumed me.

Then when I was sixteen, I started dating Cliff, the guy who would eventually become my husband. He was really the first person who recognized my obsession with weight. And he helped me realize how miserable it was making me. The main way he did that was by listening to me talk. Once I got my thoughts out of my head and into speech, I began to see how my thinking about food and my body just didn't make sense. I also started journaling. Both helped me realize how the whole body issue was controlling me.

Once I saw that, I knew I had to let go of my obsession. That was the hardest thing to do. I was so afraid it would mean getting fat. But I knew my view of my body wasn't in line with

Don't be concerned about the outward beauty that depends on fancy hairstyles, expensive jewelry, or beautiful clothes. You should be known for the beauty that comes from within, the unfading beauty of a gentle and quiet spirit, which is so precious to God.

1 PETER 3:3-4

God's view. So I began to pray that God would give me a healthy way of thinking about it.

It was a long process. It took a lot of prayer, journaling, and conversations to clear up my thinking. And honestly, there are times when I still struggle with worrying about how my body looks. But thankfully, I'm no longer controlled by it. Now I can eat a brownie and not think twice about it. That freedom is really wonderful.

THINK ABOUT IT

Danielle became overly conscious about her weight because she believed she had to look a certain way for people to like her. She admits she spent way too much time thinking and worrying about her diet. But does that mean she shouldn't have thought about it at all? How much time do you spend thinking about your weight? How can you develop a healthy, balanced perspective about eating well and exercising?

SO, WHaT NEXT?

Today's verses warn against becoming consumed with our appearance. That doesn't mean it's wrong to care about the way we look or to try to make ourselves attractive. But there are more important pursuits—like making what's on the inside beautiful.

1. Read 1 Timothy 4:8. What does this verse say about finding balance between caring for your inner and outer appearance? Which should you be more concerned about? What are some ways you can be involved in "spiritual exercise"?

2. Think about what it means to be godly. Make a list of characteristics that come to mind. Then go back and circle one trait you'd like to work on. How can you build up that trait in your life? What changes do you need to make?

3. Ask God to help you desire him and his will more than you desire physical beauty. Then read Psalm 34:5 and thank God for this promise.

Danielle Young
OF CAEDMON'S CALL

Photo by Bob Frame

JanNa LOng
OF AVALON

DID GOD WANT ME MISERABLE?

ELEVENTH GRADE WAS a devastating time for me. Up until then I had a close-knit group of girlfriends, but that year, most of them began to change. They got into drugs, sex, and a lot of other stuff I just didn't agree with.

I remember spending a lot of weekends by myself, not really having much to do because I didn't want to do what my friends were doing. Occasionally, I'd go out with them anyway—usually as the designated driver. But I always felt guilty about it.

It was a really rough time for me. I dealt with a lot of loneliness and wondered why God had allowed my friends to fall away and leave me with no one.

Throughout that time my parents would always remind me that if I was faithful to God and made the right choices, standing true in my faith, he would honor my commitment. But sometimes that wasn't enough. I wanted to fit in and feel like I belonged. Thankfully, though, when my faith was weak, my parents' rules kept me from making some dumb mistakes.

Like when all my friends were heading to the beach for a senior trip. I really wanted to go, but my mom said, "Absolutely not." I was pretty angry. Even though I knew my friends would be doing stuff I didn't agree with, I still wanted to be with them.

Looking back, I'm really glad Mom said no. It protected

The command-
ments of the
Lord are right,
bringing joy to
the heart. . . .
They are a
warning to
those who hear
them; there is
great reward
for those who
obey them.

PSALM 19:8, 11

me from a lot of stuff; I found out later that some of my friends actually got arrested on that trip.

In much the same way, I think God gives us guidelines for our own good. I don't think he's trying to ruin our fun. Like my mom, he's trying to protect us from things that could ruin our lives. Sometimes we can't see that until way down the road, but when we look back, it becomes evident that he always had our best interests in mind.

SO, WHaT NEXT?

Like Janna said, God gives us guidelines for our own good. He wants to keep us from choices that will cause us pain. He wants us to enjoy life to the fullest. That's why today's verses claim that God's laws "bring joy to the heart."

1. Read Psalm 1. What's attractive about being like the tree in verse 3? What's scary about being like the "worthless chaff" in verse 4? What will it take for you to be like the tree? How can you be a person who will "delight in doing everything the Lord wants"?

2. Think of one of God's rules that you find hard to keep or that just doesn't make sense to you. Then ask a youth leader or an older Christian to help you understand why God set the particular boundary.

3. Ask God to help you trust that his ways are best and to help you follow him with all your heart—even during those times when you'd rather do something else.

THINK ABOUT IT

When Janna's mom said no to her senior trip, Janna got angry. She thought her mom was being unfair and causing her to miss out on a lot of fun. Have you ever felt that way toward God? Eventually, Janna realized her mom was right. She saw that the "fun" her friends were having really wasn't fun after all— not with consequences like a police record! What consequences could God be trying to protect you from?

Janna Long
OF AVALON

Nice Shoes, But...

Photo by Dorian Caster

Jaci VelaSquez

DO YOU EVER THINK about what really matters to you? I do, and it's really easy for me to focus on things that don't matter.

For instance, I have a tendency to spend money like it's water. I don't think about where it's going or where it's coming from. For example, I bought this expensive pair of shoes. They were beautiful, and I was so excited!

But then I started thinking, *Wait a second, this isn't making me a better person. It's just a pair of shoes!* Yeah, they look cool, but they'll probably go out of style next week. They certainly don't matter much in the whole scope of life.

It's pretty tempting for me to think that the things I have are what make me important or worthy of love. Other people I know get their value from accomplishments or their brains.

I have this friend who's a great athlete, and he struggles not to let his game define who he is. He can get so hung up on improving his athletic abilities that it becomes his top priority. But I try to remind him (and myself!) not to get caught up with success.

It's important to remember what God values most and what he wants our lives to look like. Life isn't about cool shoes or being a great athlete. It's about who we are in Christ and what we've done to bring people to him.

In the end, I don't want to be remembered for the CDs I've made, and I sure don't want to be remembered for what I wore on my feet! I want people to remember how faithful I was, how I showed Christ in my life.

> Don't store up treasures here on earth, where they can be eaten by moths and get rusty, and where thieves break in and steal. Store your treasures in heaven.
>
> MATTHEW 6:19-20

34

When I stand in front of God, I don't want him to say, "Hey, you accomplished a lot, and you had a great pair of shoes. But I never knew you." I want him to say, "You kept your eyes on me, on the things that mattered. Well done!"

SO, WHAT NEXT?

After looking at the latest fashion magazines, it's easy to get swept away in thinking we need this or that to feel important. But how can we find our significance in God alone?

1. Read Luke 16:13. What does this verse say about how money can affect our relationship with God? Like Jaci said, sometimes it isn't money that controls us. It could be your accomplishments or athletic abilities. What other masters do you serve?

2. One way to keep "stuff" from becoming too important is to give some away. Pick some of your clothes to give to the Salvation Army or some other charity. Don't just pick things you think are ugly or you haven't worn in ages. Think about how you can make somebody's day with something special that the person might not otherwise be able to afford.

3. Thank God for how he created you. Think about what treasures you're storing on earth and in heaven. Ask God to help you discern between what you really need and just want.

THINK ABOUT IT

Jaci realized she was allowing her stuff to define her self-worth. What makes you feel important or loved? Is it good grades, trendy clothes, athletic ability, or even having a boyfriend? Jaci said she wants to be remembered as a faithful follower of Christ, not for what she wore on her feet. What do you want to be remembered for?

Jaci Velasquez

Photo by Jimmy Abegg

GinnY OwEns

THEY SAID THE MEANEST THINGS

"HEY, ARE YOU BLIND or something?"

I couldn't believe what the guy had just said. How insensitive could he be? I was so stunned that I didn't know what to say.

It wasn't the first time somebody had said something about my blindness. It started in elementary school, when kids made ridiculous comments about it. You'd think they'd grow out of it as they got older, but I didn't find that to be true.

The Lord is close to the brokenhearted.

PSALM 34:18

Sometimes, I just shrugged it off like it was no big deal. Other times, it really stung. Often, the comments would come out of nowhere, totally taking me by surprise.

I went to a pretty big high school, and the halls were always crowded. So when I walked down the hallway, I often accidentally tapped somebody with my cane—and sometimes kids would say the meanest things. Or they might just whisper and stare. Yes, I can usually tell when somebody's staring at me.

Don't get me wrong. I don't want a pity party. My life has always been busy and full, and I've always had great friends. And I'm okay with the way God made me.

But there have been some very frustrating and lonely moments, especially when I was in high school. I just wanted to be respected and accepted for who I was. It's hard enough to fit in, but when you have a disability, it makes things even harder. Seems like there's always somebody with something mean to say.

At times, I felt like God was my only friend, that he was the only constant in my life, the only one who wouldn't let me down, the only one who really knew and cared about everything I went through.

When things got difficult, I would always cling to that—knowing God was always with me, that he always saw what was going on, and that he promised to give me strength and never leave me (Deuteronomy 31:6).

I've clung to that truth many times over the years. And I still do. Always will.

THINK ABOUT IT

You can probably relate to Ginny. You've probably been stung by the insensitive words of others, so stunned that you didn't know what to say. And you've probably felt at times like God was your only friend. How did you make it through those times? Were you aware of God's presence, or did he feel silent and distant? What does today's verse mean when it says God is "close to the brokenhearted"?

SO, WHAT NEXT?

When you're feeling lonely or rejected, or like you don't have a friend in the world, you really can find peace and security in knowing that God holds you in his hand.

1. Few people have known more pain and rejection than David. Read Psalm 25:16-21. Can you relate? But even in his darkest moments, David knew God was with him. Read Psalm 3:1-5, and try to imagine God as your shield, lifting your head and bringing you comfort.

2. If you're dealing with loneliness or rejection right now, memorize Psalm 118:5-6 and cling to that promise. If you have a friend who's feeling this way, take her out for coffee or ice cream—and a big serving of encouraging words (see 1 Thessalonians 5:11).

3. You read part of Psalm 25 above. Now reread the whole psalm, this time slowly praying the words to God. In the last verse (verse 22), replace the word *Israel* with your own name.

Ginny Owens

GROWING PAINS

Photo by Kristin Barlowe

KaTy HudsOn

God is exalted
beyond what we
can understand.

JOB 36:26

WHEN I WAS RECORDING my first CD, some music people said I needed a "mission statement"—something clearly stating what I believe and why I believe it and my specific plans for my "music ministry."

I was like, "Whoa! Hold on! I'm just sixteen here, and I don't have everything all figured out yet."

I don't think I ever will have it all figured out, either. There are some things I know for sure—like God loves me and his Son, Jesus, died on the cross for me. But there are a lot more things I don't understand than things I do understand. And that's okay, because I think there are some things we're just not supposed to understand.

For me, being a Christian is a journey, a constant learning process. It's a path that includes all kinds of pits and holes you can fall into. It's a lot like that book *Pilgrim's Progress*. It's a process.

I'm okay with admitting I don't have it all figured out. That's part of the deal, I think. I talk about that in my song "Growing Pains":

> I may not have a Ph.D. or speak in
>   eloquent philosophy
> I'm nothing more than simply me, you see
> I'm still growing, still stretchin',
> Still breaking in these new shoes
> Looking for a way to make a mark of my own
> I'm just a spring chick, wet behind the ears
> It's a part of life, so there's no need to fear
> These growing pains I'm going through

I think this is what kids want to say. This is our anthem. We don't like being written off as if we don't know much about God. I haven't ever seen a limit on whom God can use.

I don't have it all figured out, but I want to share what I know and give everything I have been given, because that is what God wants me to do.

SO, WHaT NEXT?

In school we are expected to study and understand a variety of subjects. But when we study God and his Word, we come far short of understanding everything about him. But is that really a bad thing?

1. Read Job 38:1-11. What are some questions God asked Job? Could Job answer those questions? What do those questions say about God's character?

2. Look up other Scripture passages that describe God's character—like 2 Chronicles 6:41, Psalm 33:4, Proverbs 21:30, Ephesians 4:32. From those Scriptures, start a list of God's attributes—like powerful, loving, and wise. Keep the list in your Bible and add to it as you find more Scriptures that describe God's character. Write today's verse (Job 36:26) at the top of the list as a reminder that it's okay for God to be beyond your understanding.

3. Thank God for being God and for having the characteristics you've written down on your list. Ask him to teach you more about himself each day.

THINK ABOUT IT

Sometimes life is hard to understand. Katy realizes there are many things she won't understand in this lifetime, especially about God. But she holds on to what she does know—that God loves her and Christ died for her. What characteristics of God do you find hard to grasp? What truths about God do you hold on to? Katy describes the Christian life as a "constant learning process." What is God teaching you at this time?

Katy Hudson

Photo by Michael Haber

HeAther PaYne
OF POINT OF GRACE

Lazybones? That Was Me!

I GREW UP IN THE SOUTH, where it seems like all the food is fried. It tastes great, but it packs on the pounds!

I struggled with my weight for years. I wish I could blame it on all that fried food. Yes, it's fattening. But it's not the food's fault that my choir outfit just happened to be bigger than everybody else's. I had to take some of the blame myself.

When it came to eating, I just wasn't very disciplined. I'd eat whatever and not think much about it. Why? Because I liked food. I didn't want to discipline myself to eat better or to work out, because those things weren't fun.

Oh, I could be disciplined when it came to doing the things I loved. I had plenty of self-discipline when it came to music, church, and my friendships. It was easy to be serious about them.

Proverbs 6:9 says, "Lazybones, how long will you sleep?" That verse made me think of myself. I was being lazy in certain things—like eating right or spending time with God.

I eventually learned the importance of being disciplined. *Discipline* is a word we'd like to avoid. It makes us uncomfortable. It sounds like work. Which it is. But discipline is also good for us—physically, mentally, and spiritually.

I started being more disciplined about my body, eating better and working out. I haven't been overweight in a long time, and I feel much better because of it.

> Spend your time and energy in training yourself for spiritual fitness.
>
> 1 TIMOTHY 4:7

I also realized that once you're disciplined in one area, that will carry over into other areas too—like my quiet times with the Lord. I've become more disciplined there, too, spending time in the Word, in Bible study, in prayer.

As a result, I've learned the most important thing is to be satisfied in God—not in food, not friends, not studies, not sports, but God alone. Being satisfied in God alone brings glory to him and blessings to us.

THINK ABOUT IT

When you're doing something you like, it's easy to get motivated—and the time passes so quickly! But when you're doing something you don't like, or something that just seems to be a drag, it seems more like work. Wouldn't it be great if life just consisted of doing the things we love and avoiding the things we don't like? Maybe, but what would we learn? How would we grow?

SO, WHaT NEXT?

Today's verse (1 Timothy 4:7) refers to "spiritual fitness," and we all know that it takes discipline to get fit. Heather talked a lot about discipline. In what areas are you disciplined? Where do you need more discipline?

1. Read 1 Timothy 4:7-15. The passage includes words like "spiritual fitness," "work hard and suffer much," and "throw yourself into your tasks." What's your reaction to those words? The benefit? See verse 16. Now, it doesn't mean we can work our way to heaven (see Ephesians 2:8-9), but that discipline merely brings us—and others—closer to God.

2. There's no magic formula for developing discipline. You simply commit to something and then stick to it. Choose an area where you need more discipline—regular devotions, less TV, more exercise, whatever—and do it for one month. Then ask, "How have I changed because of this commitment?"

3. Ask God to help you do whatever it takes to "train yourself for spiritual fitness."

Heather Payne

OF POINT OF GRACE

WISHING FOR A REAL DAD

Photo by Robert Ascroft

LiSa KimMey
OF OUT OF EDEN

I WAS ONLY FIVE when my parents divorced. Four years later, my mother remarried. For a few years, things were okay with my new stepdad. But then he made some bad business decisions and lost a ton of money. He got bitter, turned to alcohol, and became verbally abusive. He could be really nice one minute and just awful the next.

It got so bad that my sisters and I prayed that Mom and our stepdad would break up.

Even if my father and mother abandon me, the Lord will hold me close.

PSALM 27:10

But even though I had a lousy example for a father, I never really got bitter about it. And that comes straight from God—and my mom.

My mother taught us at an early age to trust in God, to pray, to read our Bibles. She taught us that God's love is unfailing. And God showed me he could be the Father I didn't have. I learned that I could want to do the right thing to please my heavenly Father, since I didn't have the satisfaction of pleasing a natural father.

People would say, "God is the best Father you can ever have," and we didn't have any trouble believing it. We pretty much assumed that the Creator of the universe was a better father than what we'd experienced!

Still, I've had to forgive my stepdad for the way he treated our family. I've had to choose not to let bitterness get hold of me the way it had gotten hold of him. I've had to pray, "God, if it kills me, I'm going to forgive him. I'm going to trust you, and I'm going to forgive him."

That's been a process. It's not like I just forgave him one day and then moved on with the rest of my life. Memories still come back to haunt me sometimes. When they do, I have to choose between bitterness and forgiveness.

I choose forgiveness. But I can't do it without God. When you have a heart to do what God wants you to do, he helps you do it—time and time again.

SO, WHAT NEXT?

Sometimes when we experience hard times, we wonder if God knows exactly what we're going through. Does he know what it's like to feel abandoned? Yes, he does. He's been there.

1. Read Psalm 22:1-2. These anguished cries from David are also a prophetic picture of Jesus on the cross. Read Psalm 22:7-8, 14-18. All of those verses came true at the Crucifixion. Now read Matthew 27:46, which tells us Jesus knew what it felt like to be abandoned by a father. Finally, read Romans 8:15-17 for a good description of your heavenly Father.

2. Don't wait till Father's Day to do something special for your dad. Make him breakfast in bed. Wash his car. Tell him you love him. If your dad isn't at home, write God a thank-you note for being your heavenly Father, then tuck it into your Bible.

3. Read Galatians 3:26–4:7 as a prayer to God, thanking him for the benefits of being his child.

Can you identify with Lisa's story? Or maybe you have a friend who can relate? Many who have lost a father to divorce know what it's like to long for a loving dad—and Lisa says she found that in God, her heavenly Father. Do you think God can really fill the role that a loving earthly father would normally fill? How can God "hold me close," as today's verse says?

Lisa Kimmey
OF OUT OF EDEN

Photo by Mike Ruiz

KriStin SwinFord
OF ZOEgirl

TRUE GRATITUDE

DURING A MISSIONS TRIP to Venezuela, I visited an area that had been hit by a disastrous mudslide that killed thousands of people. The government wasn't offering much help in cleaning up the area or digging out the mud-filled homes, so our group stepped in to do what we could in one day's time.

Most of these homes were simply four concrete walls put together with a flat roof. Some of them were completely buried in the mud, while others were salvageable. We barely made it in the door of one home that had mud up to our waists. This would eventually be the home for a new pastor who was moving to the area.

For even I, the Son of Man, came here not to be served but to serve others, and to give my life as a ransom for many.

MARK 10:45

Once we were inside, we started shoveling. The more we dug, the more we found. It was so sad to come across the possessions of the people who once lived there. We found clothes, shoes, silverware, plates, and a TV.

While we were working, we could see people trickling down the mountain to come see what we were doing. One family that came to see our progress was so moved by what we had done, they decided to give their home (which they were moving out of) to the new pastor. Their house was bigger and even had electricity, but they were willing to give that up because they were so grateful for the help their community had received.

I was amazed by this group's thankfulness for the little work we did. We barely accomplished anything, but it was a start.

Their gratitude was very humbling. And it made me look at my own attitude. I realized how I often focus on myself rather than consider the needs of others and what I can do to serve them. When you serve, you are putting someone else's needs ahead of your own. That can be the best feeling because you know you're reaching out to someone else.

SO, WHaT NEXT?

In today's verse (Mark 10:45), Jesus says that he came to serve. As a Jesus follower, how can you have the same type of attitude?

1. Read Mark 10:35-45. What did James and John want Jesus to do for them? Why do you think they wanted that? What did Jesus mean by his response in verse 38? Later in the passage, Jesus describes what many Christians call "servant leadership." What are four or five characteristics of a servant leader?

2. Search for ways you can help out in your community, maybe through a soup kitchen or a homeless shelter. You might even look for ways to serve through taking a missions trip with your church or a Christian organization.

3. Thank God for the wonderful things he has given you—family, friends, shelter, clothes. Ask him to open your eyes to opportunities to serve others, whether it's those you know and love or whether it's a stranger.

THINK ABOUT IT
While digging out mud-filled houses in Venezuela, Kristin discovered many things that had been buried—clothes, shoes, and even a TV. A natural disaster had destroyed many homes and lives, but the Venezuelan people were still thankful for what they had and the little help they had received. How would you feel if everything you owned was destroyed? Do you take your stuff for granted? How can we become more aware of those in need?

Kristin Swinford
OF ZOEGIRL

Photo by Ben Pearson

JenniFer KnApp

*J*UST BETWEEN *M*E AND *G*OD

I CARRY MY JOURNAL with me everywhere.

Writing in it has helped me develop a firm faith and deeper relationship with God. There's nothing like going to a quiet place and fleshing out everything on my mind, even if it doesn't make sense.

That's one cool thing about journaling. It's just between you and God. It's like therapy—it's confessional, it's healing, it's redeeming.

Journaling also helps me process things better, to slow down and take time to listen to God. And it helps me retain spiritual truths because I've written them down, I've thought about them, and I've reflected on them.

I talk to God a lot in my journal. Recently, I wrote:

> I cower now at the gentle call of your spirit
> in quiet places. I grow frightened at the
> thought of your power—healing, loving,
> resurrecting. How then should I respond
> when I see your face? How could I know
> you more? What could I even begin
> to fathom?

Sometimes my journal reads like a diary. Sometimes it's like an outline of a book of the Bible. Sometimes it's more artistic, like poetry or tidbits of a song I'm working on.

I also like to read through my old journals, just to see how God worked at that time in my life. If I'm struggling with depression or self-esteem, I can go back and see how I dealt with it before—what I was thinking, what Scriptures may have helped.

As I look through old journals, it's incredible how my thought processes have changed in the last few years. My character has matured in some ways, and it has regressed in others. That's hard to admit. But that's what journaling does for you: It's kind of like looking into a mirror.

Sometimes, something from my journal ends up in a song. I don't plan it that way, but I appreciate it when it happens.

And when it does, it's kind of like the fingerprint of God, because I feel like those are his words more than mine.

THINK ABOUT IT

Jennifer is obviously a big fan of journaling. As you read her thoughts, what are some good reasons for journaling? Ask your grandparents what they remember about their teenage years. Ask if they kept a journal. If so, ask if you can read it—and see what makes it so valuable. Ask yourself, "Fifty years from now, will I wish I'd kept a journal while I was a teenager?" Why or why not?

SO, WHAT NEXT?

Jennifer sometimes reads her old journals to see how she handled situations in the past. Why is that a good idea?

1. Today's verse (Exodus 17:14) comes right after the Israelites had a great military victory. Read Exodus 17:8-15. Why did God want Moses to write it down? God told Moses to "journal" again later (Deuteronomy 31:19). Moses concluded his "journal" (Deuteronomy 32:1-47) by saying, "They are not just idle words for you—they are your life"(32:47, NIV). What does this mean for you today?

2. If you do keep a journal, put a list in it today titled "Seven Great Reasons to Keep Journaling." If you don't keep a journal, buy a spiral notebook and commit to writing in it at least three times a week for one month.

3. Reread Deuteronomy 32:1-4 as a prayer to God. Ask him to help you make it a habit to keep a journal of what he's teaching you, what you're asking him, and how you're growing in your faith.

Jennifer Knapp

JEALOUS OF MY BEST FRIEND?

Photo by Matthew Barnes

MaRgaret BeCker

I USED TO THINK jealousy was something you felt for an enemy, not a friend—at least until that night Kim and I went to a party together.

Kim was always the center of attention, and I had no problem with that. But when I tried to share a story at the party, people seemed to ignore me and pay attention to Kim instead. That's when the feeling began, a sick feeling in my stomach, somewhere between sadness and anger. The more attention Kim got, the worse I felt. I thought, *This can't be jealousy. Kim's my best friend!*

That was the first of many times I was bothered by the attention Kim received. The worst part was that I couldn't control these feelings. They controlled me.

Then I read this in my Bible: "Anger is cruel, and wrath is like a flood, but who can survive the destructiveness of jealousy?" (Proverbs 27:4). I thought about that. Anger is a raging emotion. Fury fuels wars. Of anger, wrath, and jealousy, it seems jealousy is the strongest emotion of the three.

I begged God to help me understand what was going on inside of me. I also asked myself some hard questions: How could I be so out of control emotionally? Was I afraid of losing a friendship? Afraid I wasn't cool, or afraid that Kim was better than me?

I concluded that my jealousy was all about fear. And I had to get rid of that fear.

> Anger is cruel, and wrath is like a flood, but who can survive the destructiveness of jealousy?
>
> PROVERBS 27:4

So I asked God to forgive me, to calm my fears, to help me concentrate on his opinion of me more than anyone else's. I kept asking for these things until jealousy's grip was broken.

God answered my prayer. It was tough. But in time, I found myself smiling more when Kim spoke. I found myself listening to her instead of worrying that she was grabbing everyone's attention.

I was glad for these changes. After all, jealousy is the furthest thing from love, and I want to love my best friend.

THINK ABOUT IT

Can you think of a time when you were jealous of someone? How did your jealousy affect your relationship with that person? What did you do about it? One thing about jealousy: It's our problem, and nobody else's. It's not like "righteous anger," which we can often justify because somebody has done something evil or unethical. Jealousy is never justified, and God calls it a sin.

SO, WHAT NEXT?

Margaret wrote that jealousy felt like a sick feeling in her stomach. We've all had that feeling. The question is, what does the Bible say about jealousy, and what can we do about it?

1. We sometimes think of jealousy as a minor sin, but the Bible lists it alongside stuff like "getting drunk," "sexual immorality," "idolatry," and "participation in demonic activities" (Romans 13:13, Galatians 5:19-20). Considering this, what should be our attitude toward it?

2. Margaret noted that after she prayed for a while, she began smiling at her friend more and listening more instead of seething and showing anger. Sometimes we need to take steps like this even before we feel like it. What are some practical ways you can begin to move beyond jealousy and show your friend that you care?

3. If you're jealous of someone, ask God to help you overcome it with kindness. If you're not jealous, ask God to protect you from it.

Margaret Becker

Jennifer Deibler
of FFH

Too Scared to Try!

AS A TEEN, I was terrified of singing in front of people. My parents would beg me to sing in church, and sometimes they'd even offer me money, but I refused. Singing was a secretive thing for me, something I only shared with a few people. Yet, I felt God had called me to sing in order to share his love. It didn't make sense that I was scared to do something God wanted me to do.

I remember praying at age fourteen, *Okay, God, I know you're faithful, but I don't know how you're going to do this. Are you sure that's what you want me to do?* Deep down inside, I knew the answer. I knew God had given me a gift and wanted me to use it.

Even so, I waited. I guess I was waiting for my fears to go away, but they didn't. I even wondered if singing was really what God had called me to do. *Maybe I misunderstood you. Have you chosen someone else because I was too scared to try?*

During that time, my dad told me that in order for God to steer me, I had to get moving—just like a car can't be steered if it's sitting still. Finally, at nineteen, I started moving and sang my first solo in front of my church congregation. I did it as a surprise Christmas present for my mom. I think I surprised myself more by actually going through with it.

From then on, singing in front of people got easier each time. I still get nervous now and then, but my fears don't consume me like they once did.

Through my battle with stage fright, I've learned that God

> Don't be afraid, for I am with you. Do not be dismayed, for I am your God. I will strengthen you. I will help you. I will uphold you with my victorious right hand.
>
> ISAIAH 41:10

can use anybody. If you had told me at fourteen that I'd be singing in front of hundreds of people almost every night, I would've thought you were crazy. But because I followed God's calling even when it didn't make sense, he continues to give me amazing opportunities.

SO, WHaT NEXT?

God wanted to use Moses in a major way, to free his people (the Israelites) from slavery under the Egyptians. But Moses wasn't sure how that would happen.

1. Read Exodus 4:1-16. What questions did Moses ask God about his assignment? Look at verse 10. Why did Moses feel inadequate about his assignment? What physical signs did God give Moses to use when he approached Pharaoh? What signs has God given you to get you moving? Encouragement from a friend? An answered prayer? An obvious need? Or maybe just a tugging at your heart that tells you to step out in faith?

2. Talk to a friend or family member about something God's calling you to do but you're scared to follow through on. Have that person hold you accountable to take the next step.

3. Thank God that he can use you even in your weakest moments. Ask him for strength to obey even when it's difficult.

THINK ABOUT IT

Jennifer couldn't believe God wanted her to sing in front of people since it terrified her. But sometimes God calls us to do things we aren't comfortable doing. Is God calling you to do something that seems scary? Maybe it's reaching out to that person who sits by herself at lunch. Or taking a stand for what you believe when your biology class talks about evolution. How will you allow God to use you?

Jennifer Deibler
OF FFH

I THOUGHT HE WAS THE GUY OF MY DREAMS

ChErie Adams
FORMERLY OF AVALON

> The Lord will work out his plans for my life—for your faithful love, O Lord, endures forever.
>
> PSALM 138:8

I WAS ONLY SIXTEEN when I met him, and I thought for sure he was the guy of my dreams. He played football and was great looking—all the girls at school wanted to go out with him. When we started dating, I thought I was the luckiest girl alive.

Pretty soon, my life began to revolve around him. All I wanted to do was be with him.

We dated all through high school and college, and I just knew he was the man I would marry. How could he not be when I'd invested so much in our relationship?

Unfortunately, my determination to make things work was overshadowing a big problem. He didn't show much interest in spiritual things. I mean, he'd go to church with me, and I believe he was a Christian. But God didn't seem to be a big priority in his life. When we had conversations about God, I was always the one who started them.

I think one reason we stayed together for so long was that I just wasn't willing to trust God with this part of my life. I wanted to be in control of finding my true love, rather than leaving it up to God. But eventually, God brought me to a point where I had to let go of that and just allow him to work in my life.

It was about three months before we were to be married. I just didn't have peace about our relationship. So as difficult as it was, I broke off the engagement. Marriage to this guy simply wasn't what God wanted for my life.

The months and years that followed were really hard. But slowly, I learned what it means to depend on God rather than to try to work things out on my own. And he's been so faithful. Today I'm married to one of the most godly men I've ever met.

Every day I thank God—because he knew so much better than I did what would make me happy.

SO, WHaT NEXT?

Do you believe God wants what's best for you, or do you fear what he might have in store? Some people think trusting in his plan will mean doing things they don't want to do, like going to Africa as a missionary. But remember this: God created you. He knows you better than you know yourself. So trusting him means you're putting your life in the hands of someone who knows exactly what you need.

1. Read Psalm 37:4. What are some things you "delight" in? Why? What does it mean to "take delight in the Lord"? One way is to recognize that every good thing comes from him (James 1:17). What does God promise if we delight ourselves in him?

2. Still not sure you can trust God's plan for you? Try memorizing these verses: Psalm 34:8 and Psalm 103:5.

3. Ask God to help you trust that his plan is best and to let go of your desire to be in control.

Have you ever been like Cherie—so sure you knew what you wanted that you were unwilling to see any possible problems with it? There's nothing wrong with pursuing our dreams and passions, but we should always remember that God could have a different plan than what we've envisioned. We should keep ourselves open to that possibility, trusting that he knows what's best for us and that it's far better than we could ever imagine.

Cherie Adams
FORMERLY OF AVALON

Photo courtesy of Sony

GOD DOESN'T MAKE MISTAKES

ERica Atkins
OF MARY MARY

I WAS PRETTY INSECURE back in high school. When somebody would compliment one of my friends, I'd sometimes wonder, *Well, what about me?*

It's not like people were being mean to me. I just sometimes had a hard time being content with who I was and the way I looked.

I never thought I was cute enough or that my clothes were nice enough. I never thought I knew the right people. I never felt like I did the right things to get other people to like me. There were a lot of things I didn't like about myself. I hated my legs. I hated my nose. I hated my hair.

My boyfriend at the time wasn't much help, either. He'd often say things like, "If only you'd be more like so-and-so" or "If only you looked more like her."

My insecurities continued for a long time. Then, one day a few years ago, my negative feelings about myself reached a new low. I was in my room, sitting on my bed. I had just broken up with a guy.

Right then, God spoke to my heart: *I made you who you are.*

It wasn't an audible voice, just something I realized deep inside. I had always known that, but I guess I never really claimed it fully. But at that moment, I felt like God was telling me, "You don't have to be anybody else. I made you who I wanted you to be, so make the best of what you have and enjoy who you are."

The Lord doesn't make decisions the way you do! People judge by outward appearance, but the Lord looks at a person's thoughts and intentions.

1 SAMUEL 16:7

It was exactly what I needed to learn. I had always looked to others to lift me up. I'd look to a boyfriend or a friend to tell me I was pretty or that they liked my clothes.

But I've learned that it doesn't matter what other people think. You have to feel good about yourself because you're exactly the way God wants you to be. Because God does not make mistakes.

SO, WHaT NEXT?

God doesn't make mistakes—he created you to be one of a kind. So, how do we allow God's opinion to rule our lives instead of trying to gain the approval of others?

1. Read 1 Samuel 16:1-13. What were God's instructions to Samuel about anointing the next king? What type of person did Samuel believe would be the next king? What was God's response to Samuel's assumption? What does this story tell you about how God sees each of us?

2. Make two lists on a piece of paper, one a column labeled "What Others Expect," the other a column labeled "What God Desires." How are the two lists different? What traits does God value most? Now cut the columns apart and throw away the "What Others Expect" list.

3. Using your "What God Desires" list as a prayer list, ask God to help you live in a way that's pleasing to him.

THINK ABOUT IT

Erica let other people influence how she thought about herself. Those comparisons kept her from seeing how God viewed her and what he had created her to be. It's easy to do the same thing that Erica did, letting others affect your own self-image. Think about the people who influence the way you think about yourself. What can you do to change the power others have over the way you view yourself?

Erica Atkins
OF MARY MARY

ReBecca ST. JaMes

FORGIVE EVERYTHING?

ONE OF THE HARSHEST REALITIES I've recently come face-to-face with is the large number of girls whose lives have been devastated by rape. Several girls have shared their painful stories with me.

One question they often ask is, "Why did God allow this to happen?" It's even worse when the girl discovers she's pregnant. Imagine a Christian girl in this situation. She's embarrassed and scared. Abortion isn't an option, but thoughts of it plague her. And her growing baby inside is a constant reminder of what happened. She feels anger both toward the baby and the one who hurt her.

I can't begin to imagine these girls' anguish, but I know that in any situation we can either turn toward God or away from him. Most of the girls I've met have chosen to turn toward God. If they had chosen to hold on to their pain, continued to blame God, and refused to forgive those who hurt them, they would have been inwardly destroyed.

We don't know why certain things happen to us, but we do know that we can trust God, even when he calls us to do something very difficult, like in Matthew 6:14-15: "If you forgive those who sin against you, your heavenly Father will forgive you. But if you refuse to forgive others, your Father will not forgive your sins." Forgive all the sins of others? God says, yes. Gossip? Yes. Lying? Yes. Rape? Yes. Now, that's a process that could take a long time, perhaps many years. But God calls us to

If you forgive those who sin against you, your heavenly Father will forgive you.

MATTHEW 6:14

at least begin that process, to start walking that path toward forgiveness.

Every day in our relationships, we must choose whether or not we will forgive. We decide if we will let the circumstances of life make us bitter or better. When we won't forgive others, we are, in a way, underestimating God's power. It's only God's power that allows us to forgive because we just can't do it on our own.

SO, WHaT NEXT?

Rebecca says that in order to forgive others, we have to rely on God's power. What does it mean to depend on God's power?

1. Read Matthew 18:21-35. Who does the king represent? In what ways are you like the servant who owed his king a lot of money? Why was the king so angry when he learned of the servant's actions? Think about how God has forgiven you. How should this affect your willingness to forgive others? What would a refusal to forgive say about your understanding of God's forgiveness?

2. Is there anyone you need to forgive? What's standing in the way? Choose forgiveness today. If possible, let that person know you've forgiven him or her. When it seems impossible to forgive, remind yourself of how God has forgiven you when you didn't deserve it.

3. Ask God to give you a greater understanding of what it means for him to forgive you so that you will be more willing to forgive others.

THINK ABOUT IT

Rebecca's advice to forgive others, no matter what they've done, seems almost impossible, doesn't it? How could a girl forgive someone who raped her? Does God really expect that? According to Matthew 6:14-15, the answer is yes. Why do you think God is so serious about us forgiving others? What makes forgiving others difficult? When have you found it hard to forgive? What makes forgiving others possible?

Rebecca St. James

Photo by Soren Mork

Cindy MOrgan

New School, No Friends

SUMMER WAS ENDING, and I was ready for my senior year at Claiborne County High. Finally, senior year! I knew my friends and I would have the best year yet.

Then I got some bad news: Because of my dad's job, we were moving hundreds of miles away.

I'll never forget the morning we moved. The only thing left in my room was the mattress I'd slept on the night before. I looked out the window to a rainy, dismal day—just the way I felt.

We arrived the day before school started. The next morning I awoke, eyes red from crying. I knew my friends back at my old school were having a great time. I was convinced this would be the most miserable year of my life.

Then I met my new choir teacher, Mrs. Kickasola, who insisted we call her Dorothy. In spite of my plans to like nothing about North High, I couldn't help but smile as Dorothy enthusiastically led us in vocal exercises.

Because I wasn't making any new friends, I threw myself into music and spent hours writing songs. One day after class, I asked Dorothy if she'd listen to some songs I'd written. With a broad smile, she said, "Why, of course!" Nervously, I sat at the piano and began my "performance." I wasn't sure if she liked my songs until she asked me to play them for the class. I couldn't believe it. Suddenly this new school didn't seem so bad after all.

Yet I am confident that I will see the Lord's goodness while I am here in the land of the living. Wait patiently for the Lord.

PSALM 27:13-14

It was hard to leave my old school and friends, but I now see God had a plan beyond my dreams and expectations. That year played an important role in my start in Christian music. And I even made some great friends along the way.

But the best thing of all was that I learned to take chances, to stretch myself, to look up instead of down. I found out that if I trusted God to do the unimaginable, he just might.

SO, WHaT NEXT?

Cindy didn't know if she'd like her new school or even make new friends. She felt anxious about those changes because she couldn't see the end from the beginning. So, how do we learn to trust God when we're anxious?

1. Read Philippians 4:6-7. What should we be anxious about? What can we do with our anxieties? What does God promise us in return? Reread today's verse (Psalm 27:13-14). What does this tell you about God's faithfulness?

2. Cindy's new choir teacher encouraged her songwriting. This helped Cindy see the positive side of her move to a new school. Make a list of positives God has provided during a time of change. Hang them somewhere as a reminder of God's faithfulness.

3. Thank God for the blessings he gives us during hard times of change. Ask him to teach you more about his faithfulness.

Cindy Morgan

Just a Few Words Will Do

Photo by Andrew Southam

RacHael LAmpa

AS A MUSICIAN, I often meet girls who are hurting. But I don't have much time to talk to them since it's usually a quick meeting after a concert or at a bookstore or something. That's frustrating for me, because when I see someone in pain, I want to spend time with that person to offer some encouragement.

Still, I've learned that sometimes just a few words can go a long way.

At one concert, this girl walked up to the stage and handed me a note. I put it in my pocket to read later. When I finally had time to read the note backstage, it said, "There is absolutely no one I can trust, but from your music, I know I can trust you."

Worry weighs a person down; an encouraging word cheers a person up.

PROVERBS 12:25

I hoped she would stop by to meet me after the show, and I was glad when she did. People were pushing and shoving because it was an autograph line, but I did get to hear a little more of her story. She had a terrible home life, and her mom was dying. She just had lots of problems.

There wasn't much time, and I had to say something. I looked in her eyes and said, "Just remember that you have one stable friend in your life, and that's Jesus."

Her face brightened a little bit. I believe she felt encouraged by what I'd said. She seemed to have a bit of hope after that.

I learned a lot from that meeting. Yes, it's good to spend a lot of time talking to people who are hurting. But when you

60

don't have much time, just a couple of sentences will often go a long way.

I've seen it happen a number of times, so I know it's true. Besides, God's Word tells us "an encouraging word cheers a person up" (Proverbs 12:25). It's been cool to see that in my own life.

Sometimes the simplest words are the most needed words. They can lighten up somebody's day.

Rachael realized it doesn't take much to give someone encouragement and hope. Taking a moment to say a few words to a hurting girl showed that Rachael cared about the girl's problems. What if Rachael had not looked for the girl after the concert and offered an encouraging word? How might the girl have felt? When have you allowed an opportunity to care for someone pass by because you thought you didn't have enough time?

SO, WHAT NEXT?

Hurting people cross our path every day. Sometimes it's obvious they need care; other times, they're hiding their pain. We may ask people how they are doing but rarely take the time to listen to their answer. As today's story shows, we don't have to take much time. Just a few words will do. How can we show care for others regardless of what we know about them or their situation?

1. Read Luke 10:30-35. How did the priest and Levite respond to the injured man? How did the Samaritan respond? What does this story teach us about caring?

2. Greet people you meet with a smile and see how they react. Ask those you come into daily contact with "How are you really doing?" and stop to listen to their answers.

3. Thank God for those who care for you, like your family and close friends. Ask God to give you opportunities to show care, in even the smallest ways.

Rachael Lampa

CHUBBY ANKLES

Photo by Melinda DiMauro

MELissa BrOck
OF SUPERCHIC[K]

I NEVER REALLY THOUGHT that much about my ankles until one day in tenth grade when this guy said something about them. "Chubby," he said. "You have chubby ankles."

I couldn't believe what I'd just heard. But rather than blow it off, I let his comment bother me. And keep bothering me to the point that I actually believed him. And if other people thought my ankles were chubby, well then, I must be chubby all over.

Whenever I looked in the mirror, I only saw the person with the chubby ankles. I would look at myself and not see anything good there. I didn't think I was beautiful or talented. As far as I was concerned, there was nothing good about me.

So God created people in his own image; God patterned them after himself; male and female he created them.

GENESIS 1:27

It only got worse as I looked to other things to try to define the perfect look: the media, magazines, all the things around me. And I never felt like I could possibly measure up to any of those things.

That's the way I felt for a while.

But in the last couple of years, I've begun to learn that in God's eyes, I'm beautiful. I'm beginning to recognize the beauty he's created in me. I'm finally starting to grasp a little bit of what he created when he created me.

In learning that, I can now view myself in a completely different way. God accepts me just as I am, so I can accept myself.

Don't get me wrong. It's not like magic. It doesn't just click and you feel wonderful for the rest of your life. It's a process.

Every day you have to remind yourself, "God thinks I'm beautiful. God loves me. God created me in his image."

I know what it's like to feel ugly, to feel imperfect, to feel overweight. I've been there. But now I'm starting to get a glimpse of the other side, and I really like what I see.

SO, WHaT NEXT?

It's easy to get tangled up in the lie that self-worth is based on appearance. Magazines, TV, and movies constantly reinforce that message. But God wants to transform our thinking. He wants us to see he has a purpose in shaping each of us uniquely.

1. Reread today's verse (Genesis 1:27). What does this verse tell you about your true self-image? When you get down on yourself about your looks, what are you saying about God?

2. Stand in front of a mirror. Thank God for every feature—head to toe. Then commit to spending one whole day without comparing yourself to anyone else: models, actresses, friends. When the day ends, journal how it felt to avoid the comparison trap. Try it again the next day. Keep doing it until you're convinced God's beauty standards are different from the world's, and he thinks you're a knockout.

3. Read Ephesians 2:10. Ask God to help you believe he created you the way you are with a purpose in mind.

THINK ABOUT IT
No wonder Melissa was feeling ugly and imperfect. She was judging herself by the wrong standard, one that says you aren't beautiful unless your body is a certain size and shape. Thankfully, Melissa's eyes are being opened to the truth: Her worth is not defined by her appearance. She's a treasure because she's God's creation. What about you? Do you know you're treasured by God? Do you believe he thinks you're beautiful?

Melissa Brock
OF SUPERCHIC[K]

Photo by Frank Ockenfels3

I Don't *N*eed *Y*our *H*elp!

WHEN I WAS IN HIGH SCHOOL, I tried hard to prove that I was mature and independent and didn't need anybody's help even though I'm blind. But regardless of how hard I worked to convince them, people just didn't get it.

I wore clothes my friends liked and made grades my parents liked. I had some nice achievements. But no matter what I did, I couldn't shake people's perceptions. No matter how "normal" I looked and acted, my friends in youth group often spoke to me somewhat condescendingly, treating me like I was their little sister instead of a peer.

Then there were the uncomfortable moments when I'd get ready to cross a street, and someone would try to carry me across, as if my legs didn't work. And when I dared to ask a stranger a question, I could usually expect a response that was shouted, not spoken—as if I was deaf, not blind.

After a while, I became convinced that I didn't need others' help at all, that I could do everything on my own. And sometimes I could be pretty stubborn about it.

However, as I've lived a little more life, I've had to rethink things. I do need others. Even if I don't always need their help, I've learned to be gracious and loving about receiving it as their way of reaching out to me. After all, I've been granted plenty of grace and love from my heavenly Father, so being kind to others is the least I can do.

GiNny OWens

We have all been baptized into Christ's body by one Spirit, and we have all received the same Spirit. . . . This makes for harmony among the members, so that all the members care for each other equally.

1 CORINTHIANS 12:13, 25

We all need to depend on others, not just in our everyday lives, but in our faith too. Doing things on my own to grow in my faith is fine. But I also need other believers to help me grow.

Independence? I'm all for it. But not so much that I won't lean on others for encouragement, accountability, and wisdom. According to God's Word, those of us in the body of Christ were created to love and care for each other. We all need one another.

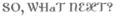

SO, WHaT NEXT?

Think about a rope used for tug-of-war. It's made up of many strands twisted together to make the rope stronger. Can you imagine playing tug-of-war with a single piece of thread? That's a picture of what it's like to stand alone.

1. Read Ecclesiastes 4:12. What does this verse say about one person standing alone? What was the writer trying to emphasize in this Scripture? Why is it important to depend on other people?

2. Start a small group with several of your close Christian friends. Your time together could be used to pray for each other, discuss what God is teaching you, and be accountable to one another. (If you're already in a small group, discuss how the group makes each of you stronger.)

3. Thank God for the people who help you grow in faith and encourage you. Ask him to remove any stubbornness or pride that keeps you from accepting help from others.

THINK ABOUT IT

Ginny longed for independence in high school. Do you feel that way? It's one thing to want independence and another to refuse dependence altogether. Have you ever refused someone's help? Why? Ginny says we need a combination of independence and dependence on our Christian journey. What are you doing to grow in faith, both on your own and with other believers? What does today's passage (1 Corinthians 12:13, 25) say about our unity as believers?

Ginny Owens

LEARNING TO LIGHTEN UP

Jennifer Knapp

This is the day the Lord has made. We will rejoice and be glad in it.

PSALM 118:24

I'VE PLAYED A LOT of concerts in amusement parks. We arrive in the morning and spend the day preparing for that night's show. But in the past, I've never taken time to ride the roller coasters.

Don't get me wrong. I love roller coasters. But I've always felt like I had to be at the stage all day, making sure every detail was perfect. I figured I didn't have time for something as trivial as a three-minute thrill ride.

Then a friend said, "You know, Jen, it wouldn't kill you to take an hour and go ride a few roller coasters. The road crew will get the stage ready. Everything will be fine. Just go out there and have some fun, okay?"

I didn't realize it at the time, but that's exactly what I needed to hear. I needed somebody to give me "permission" to lighten up and let loose.

So I took that advice and went out and rode some coasters. And I had a blast.

Sometimes it's hard for me to lighten up. I'm very driven, and I like to go, go, go. I was that way in high school and college. I'm pretty much still that way.

But I'm learning. God is teaching me that I don't have to push all the time. The Bible says, "Be still, and know that I am God" (Psalm 46:10, NIV).

God also says he'll finish what he's started in me (Philippians 1:6). Sometimes I think I have to finish everything, but God tells me to relax in his peace. He loves me because of his grace, not because of what I do—or don't do.

I have to remind myself of that. Thankfully, friends remind me too. They encourage me to stop and smell the roses, and they let me know that it's okay not to slam-dunk everything I do.

So I'm learning to lighten up.

And I'm enjoying the ride—literally—on roller coasters everywhere. I just wish the lines weren't so long!

 SO, WHaT NEXT?

Some people find it hard to relax and just enjoy time with a friend, take an afternoon nap, or even spend a couple hours riding roller coasters. Like Jennifer, many of us feel the urge to go, go, go. But even God rested after creating this entire universe, so shouldn't we also take time to lighten up and have fun?

1. Read Luke 10:38-42. What was distracting Martha? How did Mary spend her time? Are you more like Martha or Mary? Is it unrealistic to be a "Mary" all the time? Reread the verse for today (Psalm 118:24). What does it mean to rejoice and be glad in the day the Lord has created?

2. Make a list of fun things you want to do, like spending a day at the park or making popcorn and watching your favorite movie. Find time to treat yourself to something on your list.

3. Thank God for this day he created and ask him to show you new ways to enjoy it.

THINK ABOUT IT

It took a nudge from a friend to get Jennifer to take a break and just enjoy riding roller coasters. What would have to happen for you to take a break and do something different? Sometimes we get so caught up in our busyness, we forget that's not how God intends us to live. Like Jennifer said, there's a time to be still. What would our lives be like if we never slowed down?

Jennifer Knapp

**DaniElle KimmeY
OF OUT OF EDEN**

SHOULD I HANG OUT WITH HER?

I'VE ALWAYS HAD PLENTY OF friends, Christians and non-Christians. It's great to have that shared faith with Christian friends, and I always try to share my faith with my non-Christian friends.

But sometimes I have to think about how my non-Christian friends might be influencing me.

I've had this one non-Christian friend a long time. Recently I realized that I wasn't being very Christlike around her. Not that I was doing anything terribly wrong. But my faith wasn't making a difference in her life, and her lack of faith sometimes brought me down. It just wasn't a good combination when we were together.

Then it hit me: Pray for her, but don't hang out with her.

Paul tells us not to "team up with those who are unbelievers" (2 Corinthians 6:14). Paul doesn't mean we can't be friends with non-Christians. I think he just means we shouldn't become so emotionally connected to those friends that they could hurt our own walk with God. That's what was starting to happen with my friend and me.

I knew I had to make some changes. So I told my friend, "We have completely different beliefs. The way you live isn't the way I want to live. I have to live according to God's Word. When we hang out together, we're not doing what God wants us to do, so I can't keep hanging out with you."

Can two people walk together without agreeing on the direction?

AMOS 3:3

68

I'm not always that blunt; usually, I'm more tactful. But we'd been friends for years, and we've always been very honest with each other.

She understood, and we've backed off. The funny thing is, since we've stopped hanging out, she's become more interested in my faith. We talk on the phone sometimes, and I think she's considering becoming a Christian.

It doesn't always turn out that way. Sometimes the person won't be interested in faith. Sometimes the friendship might come to an end.

I still have plenty of non-Christian friends. But I'm a lot more careful about those friendships now.

SO, WHaT NEXT?

When Jesus dined with sinners, religious leaders asked, "Why do you eat and drink with such scum?" (Luke 5:30). Christ's reply—that sick people need a doctor—indicates that we, too, can bring healing to the hurting. But God's Word also implies that there are limits.

1. Read today's verse (Amos 3:3). God warned Israel about getting too close to pagan neighbors and their idols and false gods. God later said, "Come back to me and live!" (Amos 5:4). What can we learn from these verses for our own relationships?

2. Think of your best non-Christian friend. Make two lists titled, "Ways I Influence Him/Her" and "Ways He/She Influences Me." Take the list to a mature Christian—maybe a parent or pastor—and ask for advice on how to best approach that friendship.

3. Since there are no easy answers, seek God's wisdom regarding each of your non-Christian friends. Pick one of those friends today, and pray for that person—and God's direction—every day for a week.

THINK ABOUT IT

Maybe you can relate to Danielle's dilemma of wondering just how much to hang out with your non-Christian friends—and how they might be influencing you. Should you limit your time together? Only do certain things with them? Cut off the friendship completely? There are no quick and easy answers, even in the Bible. Jesus hung out with non-Christians often, and it's important for us to share our faith with unbelievers, too. But where do we draw the line?

Danielle Kimmey
OF OUT OF EDEN

Photo by Michael Haber

DEnise JoNes
OF POINT OF GRACE

Though they
stumble, they
will not fall,
for the Lord
holds them by
the hand.

PSALM 37:24

It Was All
My Fault!

NINTH-GRADE basketball. We were playing our big crosstown rival, the gym was packed, and we were down by two points when I got fouled with just a few seconds left.

I was nervous when I went to the free throw line. I had to make both shots, or we'd lose.

I took a few dribbles, eyed the basket, and shot . . . an air ball. It didn't even hit the rim. It was horrible, especially since I was usually a good free throw shooter. I don't even remember what happened with the second shot. All I knew was that we had lost, and it was my fault.

I was devastated. I was humiliated. I cried. I got home and my mom cried with me. My dad said, "You know, honey, the game wasn't lost because of you. It's a team game."

Dad was trying to encourage me, but I could not let that memory go. It destroyed my confidence. Every time I went to the free throw line for the next three years, I thought about that missed shot.

It affected more than just basketball. I became insecure, scared to step out in faith to try things. I was afraid of failing, especially in front of other people.

Those fears stuck with me for a long time, even through college and after Point of Grace had become successful. But in recent years, I've begun to let go of those fears.

I don't know why it took so long to sink in, but I finally began to understand what Jesus did for me on the cross.

Because of what he did, I am perfect in God's eyes. I'm not a failure. I've always known God loves me, but in the back of my mind, I always felt like I had to do things well—like I had to earn God's love.

I don't feel that way anymore. Now I feel free. And that's a much better feeling than making any free throw.

SO, WHaT NEXT?

Denise said she finally got over her fear of failure when she started to understand what Jesus did for her on the cross. What did she mean by that? How does Christ's crucifixion erase our fear of failure?

1. Read Romans 8:1. What does it mean that there is "no condemnation" for Christians? How does that knowledge make you free? Now read Romans 8:31-39. Compared to a missed free throw— or any other failure—this passage puts everything in perspective.

2. Read today's verse again (Psalm 37:24). Think of someone you know who has stumbled. How can you be God's "hand" to that person, to keep him or her from falling into fear, into discouragement, into depression? Do something practical to help that person this week.

3. Using Romans 8:31-39 as a guide, thank God for all his marvelous promises, for his forgiveness, for his great love, for the hope he brings.

Have you ever felt like Denise? Maybe your failures aren't as public as Denise's—in front of a packed gym. Maybe your failures have been more private. In any case, when we fail, we're often afraid to get up and try again. We're afraid we'll mess up, afraid of what someone might think. We don't want to disappoint anyone, least of all ourselves. So how do we get over it and move on?

Denise Jones

OF POINT OF GRACE

WHERE ARE YOU, GOD?

NaTalie LaRuE OF LaRue

I RECENTLY WENT THROUGH a time when I felt like God had abandoned me.

I could really relate to the bride in the Song of Solomon when she said of her lover, "He was gone. I yearned for even his voice! I searched for him, but I couldn't find him anywhere. I called to him, but there was no reply" (5:6).

That's exactly how I felt. It was overwhelming.

My mom noticed something was wrong. She said, "Natalie, you're not yourself right now. What's going on?"

I told her everything. She pointed me to the Psalms and reminded me how David often grew closer to God in his times of desperation.

Mom was right. How many times was David in the wilderness, in the desert, crying out to a God who didn't seem to answer? That's what I had to do too.

I think I had reached a point where I was so comfortable in my walk with God that I just needed a little shaking up. Maybe that's why God seemed so distant.

It's like I'd been in a beautiful, wonderful valley. Everything was going so well. But I fell asleep in that valley, and when I woke up, God wasn't in the valley anymore. He was up in the mountains, and he challenged me to go to a higher point in my relationship with him. I could almost imagine him saying, "Come up to where I am. It's better up here. It's more beautiful up here. It's a better view. You'll have a better perspective."

My God, my God! Why have you forsaken me? Why do you remain so distant? Why do you ignore my cries for help?

PSALM 22:1

And that's what I started doing, climbing the mountain—through reading his Word, through prayer, through my desperate cries for help. He heard my cries, and he's helped me continue my trek up the mountain.

Things are much better now, but I'm still climbing. Because God is incomprehensible, I'll never reach the top—at least not until I get to heaven.

But I sure am enjoying the journey a lot more.

THINK ABOUT IT

Can you relate to Natalie's story? Have you ever felt like God has abandoned you? Sometimes when we feel that way, the last thing we want to do is dig into our Bibles or spend time in prayer. But that's exactly what God calls us to do—even when he seems distant, even when he seems like he's not listening at all. He calls us to begin climbing the mountain, to keep seeking his face.

SO, WHAT NEXT?

Natalie mentioned David and the Psalms, and how she could identify with his "wilderness times." Jesus could also identify. Today's verse (Psalm 22:1) is not only David's cry for help but also Christ's very words on the cross.

1. Read Psalms 6:2-4, 13:1-3, 17:1, 27:9, and 55:1. Do you see a pattern here? There are many more examples throughout the Psalms that show David feeling abandoned and crying out to God. But God always answered. Psalm 40 is one of his most beautiful answers. Check it out.

2. Memorize the first three verses of Psalm 40 or write them on a card and tape them to the inside of your locker. Lean on those truths in times when you're feeling abandoned.

3. Psalm 40 is also a marvelous prayer. Read the words aloud to God, pausing for a moment after each verse to meditate on its significance and thanking him for answering your prayers.

Natalie La Rue
OF LaRUE

AliSa GiRard
OF ZOEGIRL

PAYING THE PRICE FOR FAITH

THROUGHOUT MY LIFE I've found myself surrounded by inner-city ministry. Even my home church in Los Angeles is located in the inner-city area of Echo Park.

At my church it's pretty common to see youth leaders working with gang members and runaway teens, but something happened one night that I'll never forget. I went to church for choir practice and saw this young teen girl who looked like she'd been beaten. Her face was so bruised and swollen that she was almost unrecognizable.

I walked over to one of the youth leaders and asked what had happened to this girl. She said, "Last Sunday that girl came to church and became a Christian. She decided she wanted to get out of the gang that she belonged to, so she had to go through the process and pain of getting 'jumped out.'"

Getting "jumped out" meant she had to go back to her gang, tell them she wanted out, and get beaten to a bloody pulp in order to be allowed out and left alone in the future. That's the ugly reality of gang life.

So there she was, her face bruised and swollen. But what really struck me was her smile. After all of that pain, her smile still lit up the entire room. You could tell that she was thankful to be alive, that she was joyful about her new relationship with Christ.

> It is God who gives us, along with you, the ability to stand firm for Christ. He has commissioned us, and he has identified us as his own by placing the Holy Spirit in our hearts as the first installment of everything he will give us.
>
> 2 CORINTHIANS 1:21-22

This girl paid a physical price for what she believed in. I was definitely humbled by her commitment, by the price she was willing to pay.

When some people come into contact with teens from the inner city, they see trouble coming. But I see possibilities. They may see someone to be afraid of, or someone who will never amount to anything. But I see great potential for who that person can become with Christ.

I'm reminded of this girl and how she stood firm in her faith. She was willing to accept whatever would come in order to remain joyfully devoted to Christ.

SO, WHaT NEXT?

The apostle Paul wrote a second letter to the church in Corinth to encourage believers to live out their faith joyfully. How can we follow Paul's advice and take a stand for Christ?

1. Read 2 Corinthians 1:21-24. What does it mean to "stand firm for Christ"? When have you had to take a stand? What happened as a result? What does it mean that the Holy Spirit is "the first installment of everything he will give us"? What is Paul's ultimate hope for the believers in the Corinthian church? How does this hope apply to you?

2. Try smiling at everyone you meet and see what kind of reaction you get. You might just get the opportunity to share that your joy comes from Christ alone.

3. Thank God for sending his Son that we may experience true joy. Ask him to help you endure whatever may come when you take a stand for your faith.

Alisa Girard
OF ZOEGIRL

I Wish I Hadn't Said That

DAnielle Young
OF CAEDMON'S CALL

[T]he tongue
is a small
thing, but what
enormous
damage it can
do. A tiny spark
can set a great
forest on fire.
And the tongue
is a flame of
fire.

JAMES 3:5-6

I GUESS IT'S PRETTY typical for moms and daughters to have problems during the teen years. For my mom and me, the trouble started during my senior year of high school.

Basically, we'd get into arguments because I was so sensitive about having my independence. I felt like I didn't have any at all. And so I'd blow up, even over really petty things.

For example, I remember one Sunday morning I didn't get up in time to go to Sunday school. I just went to the worship service later that morning. That afternoon, I was walking up the stairs to my bedroom when I overheard my mom talking to my dad. She made some comment about me "skipping" Sunday school, and it infuriated me.

I came running down the steps and into the room where they were. I shouted, "I heard every word you said!" Then I just let her have it. I never even mentioned Sunday school. It was straight to, "You know, you never let me have any independence at all. I can make my own decisions. I'm seventeen years old. This is ridiculous!"

I know I said a lot of hurtful things to my mom that year, things that I now definitely regret. I wish I hadn't been so selfish. I wish I could've climbed into her shoes just for a second and thought about how I was making her feel. I see now that it was probably pretty hard for her to let go and let me grow up.

If I'd taken time to think about it, I would have been a little more patient and understanding with her.

My mom and I have a great relationship now. Thankfully, that's what forgiveness is all about. But if I could do it all over again, I would definitely be more careful about choosing my words.

SO, WHaT NEXT?

As today's verse says, words have power. They can build up or tear down. That's why it's so important to think before we speak. But what should we think about? Paul offers some good suggestions in his letter to the Philippians.

1. Read Philippians 2:3-4. What would it mean to consider your parents "better than yourself"? (Check out Romans 12:10 for a clue.) How could that kind of attitude affect the way you treat them?

2. Take one or both of your parents out to lunch or for a cup of coffee this weekend. Decide beforehand that you will not be responsible for making the conversation take an ugly turn, but that you will show respect and love. Tell your parents what's going on in your life and ask about what's happening in theirs. Remind them that you love and appreciate them.

3. Ask God to help you try to understand where your parents are coming from and to be more patient with them.

THINK ABOUT IT

What's your relationship like with your parents? At this time in your life, you may be focused on the things about them that irritate you. You may find yourself rolling your eyes at them and thinking, *They just don't understand*. But wait a minute. Before you let your feelings shine through in the way you treat them, take some time to do what Danielle wishes she'd done: Put yourself in their shoes.

Danielle Young
OF CAEDMON'S CALL

Photo by Michael Gomez

Paige

My Friend's Messing Up

MY SOPHOMORE YEAR, I had a really good friend. We did everything together. She was a strong Christian and a leader in our youth group at church. A lot of people looked up to her.

But the summer after our sophomore year, she went down the wrong path, to put it mildly. She got into some bad stuff—drinking, drugs, anything you can imagine. It was a shock to everyone who knew her.

I didn't know how to handle the situation, how to hold her accountable for what she'd done and yet still be her friend and still love her. It was a struggle for me. I just prayed and prayed for her, because I didn't know what else to do.

I ended up writing a song for her, "Here in the Light." Basically, the song just says, "I don't know how to get you back to God, so I'm just going to pray for you and love you and trust God. And one day, he'll bring you back home, into the light."

Finally, I decided to talk to my friend. I went to her house and said, "I don't know everything that's going on in your life. I just want you to know I love you and I'm praying for you, and if there's anything I can do . . ."

I didn't want to be preachy, because she knew all the Christian answers. She didn't need that. She just needed somebody who could love her and accept her. We hugged, but it wasn't like, "Okay, everything's better now." It wasn't the ultimate movie ending by any means.

A friend is always loyal, and a brother is born to help in time of need.

PROVERBS 17:17

A friend is always loyal

Then I gave her a tape of my song and asked her to listen to it. She called me later, and she was pretty emotional about it.

Since then, she's slowly been taking small steps toward coming back to God. She's still struggling, though. But I'm glad I talked to her, just to let her know I'm still her friend, no matter what.

SO, WHaT NEXT?

There are few things more heartbreaking than watching a Christian friend fall into sin. When that happens, what are we supposed to do?

1. When a friend sins, sometimes God wants us to lovingly confront that friend (Matthew 18:15). But if a friend already knows she's messed up, sometimes our highest calling is simply to love her. Read the following Proverbs for some good words on being a loving friend: 3:27-28, 18:24, 27:9.

2. Write a note of encouragement to a struggling friend, whether your friend's hard times were brought on by poor choices or not. (A great example of an encouraging note: Ephesians 1:15-20.)

3. Keeping the above Scriptures in mind, ask God to show you how you can help a hurting friend. Admit to God that you, like your friend, are capable of falling on hard times. Ask God to protect you from that and to help you make wise decisions that are pleasing to him.

THINK ABOUT IT

Have you ever watched a Christian friend make bad decisions? Did you feel like you could do anything about it? Maybe, like Paige, you've felt pretty helpless. But here's the key: Paige did what she could do. For her, that meant writing a song and going to her friend's house to say she loved her. For you, that might mean a note, a phone call, an e-mail. How can you reach out to your friend today?

*R*un *A*way!

I RAN INTO AN OLD FRIEND at a grocery store one day, and as soon as I looked into her eyes, I knew something was wrong.

She later told me she'd just found out she was pregnant. She was unmarried, in college, and pursuing her dream of being a doctor. But she'd gotten involved with this guy, and when she found out she was pregnant, she found herself facing a future of raising a child without a husband to help.

She ended up quitting school to have her baby. She put the baby in day care so she could go back to school, but as a struggling single mom, her dream of being a doctor seemed swallowed up by 2 A.M. feedings and diapers that needed changing.

She was nineteen.

The consequences of premarital sex can be huge, as they were for my friend. Pregnancy and disease, including AIDS, are obvious consequences. But the emotional costs can be just as great. The Bible says when you have sex with someone, you become one with that person (Genesis 2:24). And when that's ripped apart, a piece of you stays with that person.

I've heard many stories from girls who so regret having premarital sex. I've never heard anybody say, "I'm so glad I had sex outside of marriage." They always say, "Please tell people not to go through what I've been through."

So I'm committed to saving myself for marriage—not just because of these stories, but because that's God's plan. Sex is a

Photo by Kristin Barlowe

ReBecca St. JAmes

Run away from sexual sin! No other sin so clearly affects the body as this one does. . . . Honor God with your body.

1 CORINTHIANS 6:18, 20

beautiful thing, created by God. But he created it only for marriage.

I look forward to sharing my whole self with my future husband someday. But for now, I stay out of situations where I might be tempted sexually. If I think I'm even getting close to a situation like that, I remember that the Bible tells us to run away from temptation. That's not cowardly; that's the right thing to do.

I also always remember that God is watching. And finally, I think of my future husband. I want to be able to tell him everything I've done, without shame. That's a pretty good guideline!

SO, WHaT NEXT?

Have you ever been in a tempting situation but thought, *I can handle it. I'll be strong*? What's wrong with that thinking?

1. Read Genesis 39:6-12. How did Joseph react to being seduced? What can you learn from Joseph about dealing with sexual temptation? Now reread today's verse (1 Corinthians 6:18). Does advice get any clearer than that?

2. At the top of a sheet of paper, write, "Practical Ways to Stay Pure." Starting with the passages above and adding your own ideas, make a list of strategies for remaining abstinent. Some of them will be things you do ("Avoid being alone with my boyfriend") and some will be things you know ("God is always watching me").

3. Ask God to put sort of an "alarm" in your mind that goes off any time you're even getting close to sexual temptation. Ask him to sound that bell before you are tempted—and to give you the strength to run away.

Maybe you know someone who has had premarital sex and regrets it. Maybe you've been there yourself. God's forgiveness is more than big enough to make you whole again (see 1 Corinthians 6:9-11; 1 John 1:9). Or maybe you're like Rebecca, committed to remaining sexually pure until your wedding day. Rebecca mentioned a few strategies for keeping her commitment. What about you? Do you have a plan for practicing purity?

Rebecca St. James

ChRissy ConWay
OF ZOEGIRL

SHE WAS ONLY SEVENTEEN

AS A TEEN, I took chances with my life and thought I'd be fine. I got involved in partying and hanging out with the wrong crowd, which I now regret. Looking back, I'm very fortunate to be alive.

When you're seventeen, you don't usually think, *I might not be here tomorrow.* You believe you're invincible. That's something I realized years later when I found out that a seventeen-year-old girl from my hometown in New Jersey had been killed in an auto accident.

> How do you know what will happen tomorrow? For your life is like the morning fog— it's here a little while, then it's gone.
>
> JAMES 4:14

She had waited, like every other teen in New Jersey, until she turned seventeen to get her license. Now, that's a long time to wait. So when you finally get your license, it feels like you've been handed the key to freedom and that life can really begin. You're not thinking about the responsibilities or dangers that come with driving a car. You're certainly not thinking that you might not be alive the next day.

Nothing like this had happened in my small town of Mt. Ephraim. We had never experienced the death of someone so young. I'm sure she had plans for that weekend and a vacation scheduled for the summer, but none of it ever took place.

That's the reason we wrote the song "Forever 17" from the perspective of the girl who died. The words remind us that life is so very precious, and we never know when it might end:

Could I have just one more day
A chance to learn from my mistakes?
In a matter of a moment
Life fell before my eyes
And now I'm looking at the meaning of
The miracle of life
Where are we going without even knowing
The answer deep inside
So don't give up
You haven't lived yet
You're only seventeen

We only have today and can't be confident that we'll see tomorrow. So why say we'll follow God later, when we can follow him now?

The seventeen-year-old girl from Chrissy's hometown had no idea that soon after getting her license, she'd be killed. She probably thought she had her whole life ahead of her. Have you ever felt like that? It's hard to imagine life ending so abruptly, especially when you're young. Maybe you know of someone your age who has died recently. How did that make you feel? Did you make any changes in your own life as a result of that death?

SO, WHAT NEXT?

If you knew you'd die tomorrow, what would you do today? Spend it with family and friends? Do something you've always wanted to do? Since we don't know how long we have on earth, we need to think seriously about how we can fully live each day.

1. Read James 4:13-17. What type of long-term plans were the people in this passage making? How did the writer respond to their plans? According to verse 15, how should people talk about their plans? What are some of your long-term plans?

2. Think of one thing you know you should do but have been putting off for some time. Commit to doing it within the next week. And don't take no for an answer—not even from yourself!

3. Thank God for this day he's given you. Ask him to guide you and give you discernment in how you can best spend your time.

Chrissy Conway
OF ZOEGIRL

EVERYTHING I WANTED TO BE

Photo by Robert Ascroft

NiCole C. MUllen

GROWING UP, I wasn't what you'd call a really cute kid. I would call it "beauty challenged." But that sure wasn't true of Celia, an older woman I'd met at church. I thought she was the most beautiful woman I'd ever seen. But more than that, she was a very talented singer and everything I wanted to be. Sometimes I would stop at her house for a visit, and she would fix my hair, or we would practice singing together. I remember her saying, "You've got a real talent there. Let's work on your singing." While I don't think she realized it, her encouraging words and caring heart helped me in so many ways.

When I'd hear someone on the radio and decide to be like them, Celia would encourage me to be myself and pursue my dreams. She helped me realize I couldn't be another singer's carbon copy—and that I shouldn't try to be. I need to be the best "me" I possibly can.

Celia saw my talent and helped me to develop it. I'm forever grateful for her gentle encouragement, which helped bring me to where I am today. She didn't know the impact she was having on my life just by being nice and showing genuine love. She taught me what it means to have a Christlike love.

Today I mentor a group of teen girls who want to be like me. We aren't related, but they do feel like my little sisters. I love spending time with them, hanging out or going to the

And you should follow my example, just as I follow Christ's.

1 CORINTHIANS 11:1

mall. They tell me their problems, and I have to be a good listener before I give them advice. But I have to watch what I say to them and be careful with their hearts. To put it another way, I need to do for them what Celia did for me.

Being a Christlike example isn't easy, but there's always something I can do. Ultimately, I need to show them the love of God—something I can do through little acts of kindness and words of encouragement.

SO, WHaT NEXT?

All people have someone they want to be like, for whatever reason. But wanting to be like other people can be a good or bad thing, because people aren't perfect. That's why we must ultimately look to Christ.

1. Read 1 Corinthians 10:31—11:1. How does Paul encourage the Corinthians to be Christlike examples? What does Paul mean by trying to do "what is best for them so they may be saved"? Who was Paul's example? How was Christ the ultimate example (see Matthew 27:45-54)? Why is it important to have Christian role models? How can we become better examples for those who look up to us?

2. Think of someone in your life who's a positive role model. Write a note thanking that person for what you've learned by watching his or her life.

3. Thank God for sending his Son, the ultimate example, to teach us about true love. Ask him to help you become more Christlike each day so you can be a good example for those who are watching you.

Nicole C. Mullen

Photo by Ben Pearson

Jennifer Knapp

Getting Past My Selfishness

I SORT OF HAVE a love-hate relationship with missions trips. I know it's selfish, but I always start out dreading them because they're so physically and emotionally demanding. I do them anyway, though, because I feel like God calls me to.

As much as I gripe beforehand, when it's all over, I have no regrets. Why? Because, despite my selfishness, I've seen God's hand time and again, all around the world.

> Don't be selfish; don't live to make a good impression on others. Be humble, thinking of others as better than yourself.
>
> PHILIPPIANS 2:3

Like that time in Estonia. We'd just arrived after twenty hours of travel, and the airline had lost our luggage. I was hot, sweaty—and ticked. But I still had a concert that night in the town square.

So I go out there, still angry, and I start singing. A woman approaches me. She's dirty and smelly, and I'm totally repulsed by her. But she puts her hands on my face, kisses my cheek, and says something in Russian. I just want her to go away.

Somebody later translated the woman's words for me: "My daughter," she said. "You look like my daughter. I love you, I love you."

Then the words of Jesus hit me right between the eyes: "When you did it to one of the least of these . . . you were doing it to me" (Matthew 25:40). I hadn't thought of that Scripture in ages. But there it was, staring me in the face—touching me, kissing me, speaking to me in a language I couldn't understand.

It was as if I'd been touched on the face by God, and he was saying, "I'm just as much a part of this woman as I'm a part of you."

That's why I go on missions trips and seek ways to serve here at home. There are needs everywhere. And God can use every one of us, even selfish ones like me, to reach those who need a taste of his love.

Sometimes I just have to invest myself in others despite myself. Love is a choice. It's also an investment that's worth the effort.

SO, WHAT NEXT?

We all experience times when we don't feel like doing things we know we should. How do you respond in times like that? When it comes to serving, Jennifer says it's always worth it in the end. How can looking forward to that outcome help you make good choices now?

1. Read Hebrews 12:2. Then think about the agony Jesus experienced as he was brutally beaten and crucified. Knowing he would face such torture, do you think he felt like serving in this way? What was the "joy he knew would be his afterward"? (See Luke 15:4-7.) When it comes to helping others, what do we have to look forward to?

2. For the next week, serve one person in some way each day. How can setting a goal help you sidestep the "I-don't-feel-like-it" hurdle?

3. Pray that God's love will become more real to you so that it will motivate you to serve others.

Jennifer admits she struggles with self-ishness when it comes to serving others. She says serving sometimes seems like too much work. What keeps you from serving? Are you too busy doing things for yourself? Are you afraid it might make you uncomfortable? How can you move past these barriers? On Jennifer's missions trip, she was reminded that serving others is the same as serving Christ. How could that perspective motivate you to serve?

Jennifer Knapp

But I'm Too Young!

Photo by Matthew Barnes

JOy WilliaMs

Don't let anyone think less of you because you are young. Be an example to all believers in what you teach, in the way you live, in your love, your faith, and your purity.

1 TIMOTHY 4:12

I'VE ALWAYS BEEN drawn to the Bible stories in which God uses somebody young to do his work. The stories of David, Samuel, and Mary have always meant a lot to me.

At the same time, I used to think, *Yeah, but those are just Bible characters. That's not me. God couldn't use me like that.* I used to think I'd have to wait until I was old before things would really start happening.

But in the last couple of years, I've come to understand that God can use me now. And not just with my music, though that's certainly a part of it. God can use me in my everyday relationships to make a difference for him.

To me, that's an amazing thought—that God would use me, a regular Joe Schmoe, a teenager. But it makes me nervous, too. A while back I was scheduled to sing at a luncheon for some people in the music industry. The whole morning before the luncheon, I was a wreck just thinking about it. It felt like a huge weight on my shoulders.

Then I realized I just needed to trust God, to give him my worries, and to know that he would use me—just like he'd used David, Samuel, and Mary. He gave me my voice, and I want to use it for him, even though I'm so not worthy. I'm incredibly humbled by it all.

I might be young, but I want to be a good steward of what God has given me. Not just with music, because my voice could be gone someday. But I want to reflect God with my whole life.

88

I want to "set an example for the believers in speech, in life, in love, in faith and in purity" (NIV), as today's verse says. I just pray I will represent God well in everything I do.

SO, WHaT NEXT?

Maybe you can't make CDs and perform in concerts all over the place like Joy Williams. But you do have an audience every day—your family, your friends, your neighbors. Do they see you being an example of faith?

1. Read 1 Samuel 16:1-13. Samuel assumed God had chosen one of Jesse's older—and taller and stronger—sons to be king. But Samuel was wrong; God chose David, the youngest and smallest. Reread verse 7. How does this passage encourage you? What qualified David for the job? For a clue, see Deuteronomy 6:4-6.

2. Ask three adults who know you well, "What do you think I do well? How can I use that to put my faith into action?" Then take one of their suggestions and go for it!

3. Read Psalm 71:17, and note David's words about his youth. Now read Psalm 71:14-17 as a prayer.

THINK ABOUT IT

"Just wait till you're older." Have you ever heard those words? It's often good advice; you'd say that to an eleven-year-old who wants to drive a car, for instance. But as today's verse says, you're never too young to be an example. Joy says it took her a while to realize that God could do big things through her, even as a teenager. How about you? What exciting plans might God have for you, right now?

Joy Williams

I Was So Hateful

MY SISTER ROBYN and I are like best friends, but I couldn't always say that. When I was in junior high and high school, our relationship wasn't that great. And it was totally my fault.

Robyn is eight years younger than me. She wanted to go everywhere with me. But when you're fourteen or fifteen, you don't exactly want your six- or seven-year-old sister tagging along. For me, it was like, "Bye bye." I never let her go anywhere with me and my friends.

Photo by Michael Haber

ShElley BReen
of Point of Grace

Those who bring trouble on their families inherit only the wind.

PROVERBS 11:29

I remember one time when my cousins and I were spending a weekend at my grandpa's house. We were so mean to Robyn. We didn't do anything with her the whole weekend, and we kept calling her names. She cried, but we were like, "We don't want to play with you." I was so hateful. It kills me even to think about it now.

I don't know why people sometimes feel like they can treat their siblings like dirt. If we treat our friends like that, they won't stick around. So why do we treat our siblings like that? Is it because we know they're not going anywhere?

Now, I realize that's the very reason we should treat them with respect, because they are going to be with us for the rest of our life. Unfortunately, I didn't realize that until I was in college. That's when I suddenly realized Robyn was no longer just a little sister who always wanted to follow me around. We'd reached the point where we were finally on the same level and we could talk about stuff.

Now, our relationship is awesome. We do lots of things together.

I wish somebody had told me back then, "You know, someday you're going to feel really bad about the way you've treated your sister. Can't you just give her a little bit of your time?"

I wish now that I had done that. Because just a little bit of my time would have gone a long, long way.

SO, WHaT NEXT?

Fortunately, Shelley and her sister get along just great these days. But because of the way Shelley treated Robyn back then, they lost some years of what might have been a great relationship. Are you missing out on a good relationship because of your actions?

1. Read today's verse (Proverbs 11:29). Are you bringing "trouble" to anyone in your family? How could you change that? Now read the next verse (Proverbs 11:30). How can you "bear life-giving fruit" to your family? What does that fruit look like? (See Galatians 5:22-23 for some suggestions.)

2. Pick a relationship with a family member that needs some work. Think of one thing you can do this week to improve that relationship—even just a little—and then be sure to do it.

3. Ask God to help you to avoid bringing trouble on your family and to be a person who brings life-giving fruit.

THINK ABOUT IT

When Shelley recalls her junior high and high school days, she has many regrets about how she treated her little sister. She wishes she had known then what she knows now: That siblings are forever, and that they deserve our love and respect all along. It's hard to look to the future, but ask yourself: "Ten years from now, will I regret the way I'm treating anyone in my family today?"

Shelley Breen
OF POINT OF GRACE

91

ONE REALLY TOUGH QUESTION

Photo by Bob Frame

JAnna Long
OF AVALON

WHEN I WAS ABOUT FIFTEEN, my dad pulled me aside for a pretty serious conversation.

He said, "I know you're going to be dating soon, Janna, and I just want to go over some things with you that are close to my heart."

He basically just encouraged me to remain a virgin. He explained that God had set up certain guidelines—like forbidding premarital sex—to keep us from getting hurt. And that one day God would bring me the person I was supposed to marry.

I nodded in agreement, not at all expecting what he would say next.

"If you ever get close to rethinking your decision to remain pure," he said, "I want you to know that on the day you get married, or sometime before, I'm going to sit down and talk with you, and I'm going to ask you if you're a virgin. And you'll have to answer me.

"Anytime you think about giving yourself to someone," he continued, "I want you to remember this talk, and remember that I trust you will never lie to me."

I remember walking out of the room after we'd finished talking, thinking how awful that would be for me to have to tell my dad thirty minutes before my wedding, while we're standing in the bride's room, "By the way, I'm not a virgin anymore."

I have to say, if for no other reason, that conversation kept me from having sex before I got married. I mean, I know if I

Obey your spiritual leaders and do what they say. Their work is to watch over your souls, and they know they are accountable to God. Give them reason to do this joyfully and not with sorrow.

HEBREWS 13:17

92

had messed up, my dad would have forgiven me and shown me grace and love. But thinking about how disappointed he would be was such a powerful motivator. Any time I was tempted to compromise my standards, I thought about that.

Now that I'm married, I can definitely say it was worth the wait. I can also thank my dad for holding me accountable. What a blessing!

SO, WHaT NEXT?

Having someone hold you accountable means having that person ask you whether you're following through with commitments you've made—anything from daily devotions to sexual purity. Who could play that role for you?

1. Read today's verse (Hebrews 13:17). How did Janna's dad play the role described in the verse? Why is it important to have someone to "watch over your soul"? By remaining pure, Janna gave her dad reason to hold her accountable "joyfully and not with sorrow." How would that type of accountability help you in your walk with God?

2. If you already have someone who's holding you accountable, thank that person today with a note, a "date" for coffee, or a gift certificate to a favorite bookstore. If you don't have such a person, begin thinking about who could be that person for you.

3. Pray for the person who's holding you accountable, asking God's blessings upon him or her today. If you don't have such a person, ask God to provide one.

THINK ABOUT IT

Some might disagree with the way Janna's dad handled his talk with her. But Janna says it helped her make a commitment she was later very thankful for. By saying he would ask her about her virginity before her wedding, Janna's dad was providing accountability for his daughter. Do you have anyone in your life who's willing to ask you hard questions? Such a person can play an important role in helping you live for God.

Janna Long

OF AVALON

Photo by Dorian Caster

Jaci Velasquez

*W*hat's *W*rong with *M*e?

NEVER FEEL LIKE nobody likes you? I feel that way sometimes, too. I think it's natural to want to be liked. I mean, who doesn't want friends? But I struggle with wanting everyone to like me. And when they don't, it's easy for me to feel bad about myself.

I have this big group of friends, and in that group, there's one girl who hangs out mostly with the guys.

Now, I was raised with brothers, and I usually feel more comfortable hanging around with guys than with girls. And most of the time, guys feel comfortable hanging out with me, too. So it kind of hurt that the guys were hanging out with this other girl and not with me.

One day, it really started to bother me—enough to make me cry. I was like, "What's wrong with me? Am I not sweet enough? Am I not likable?" I came up with all these reasons why people wouldn't want to hang out with me. For instance, I have a strong personality. I'm also very honest and say what's on my mind, which isn't always the best thing. I figured if I changed, people might like me better.

After my crying session, I decided I would try to be sweet and quiet—the kind of girl everyone would love. But that just wasn't me. Then it hit me: People want to be with whom they want to be with. My guy friends didn't hate me. They were just hanging out with another person. That's the way life works.

The Lord will not reject his people; he will not abandon his own special possession.

PSALM 94:14

94

I've learned that not everyone is going to love me. Not everyone will always want to be around me. That doesn't mean there's something wrong with me or with them. People are just different. Sure, there are things about me that I need to work on. But I don't have to try to be everyone's best friend. I only need to be the person God made me to be.

SO, WHaT NEXT?

If we try to be everyone's best friend, as Jaci says she's sometimes tempted to do, we become focused on living for others, doing whatever it takes to make them like us. One problem with that is we end up pretending to be something we're not, which will ultimately make us miserable. An even bigger problem is that we make the opinions of others a bigger priority than living for God.

1. Read Galatians 1:10. Then think about the way you live. By your actions do you show that you're more concerned with God's approval or your peers'?

2. Look up Zephaniah 3:17, and write it down on a note card. Remind yourself often of how God rejoices over those who are in Christ.

3. Pray that God will help you grasp his overwhelming love for you. Ask him to help you find security in the way he views you, rather than caring too much about what others think.

THINK ABOUT IT

If someone doesn't seem to like you, what's your response? What's the danger in caring too much about what others think of you? There's nothing wrong with wanting people to like you. The problem comes when you let their feelings about you affect the way you feel about yourself. What makes someone else's opinion of you so important anyway? Remember that as a Christian you have God's complete approval, and he thinks you're incredible. Whose opinion could matter more?

Jaci Velasquez

It All Started at Church

Photo by Robert Ascroft

Andrea Baca
of Out of Eden

WHEN I WAS NINETEEN, I was getting tired of singing with Out of Eden. It was getting to be a drag. So I was like, "Lord, what do you want me to do with my life?"

Then we went on a retreat with some pastors from our church, and I realized what I was really missing: Church. We were on the road so much, we rarely had a chance to attend our church. And when we did go, we weren't very involved.

One of my pastors said, "You need to get under spiritual authority, and you need to serve in your church." He was right: I needed someone—like my pastor—to teach me and help me grow in my faith. And I needed to get involved, working with the nursery or the youth group or something else.

In the next year, we had a lot of time off, and we went to church a lot more. It felt great to be plugged in again. I not only grew in my faith, but I also grew more confident in the gifts and abilities God had given me.

Before then, I hardly ever talked onstage at our concerts. My sisters did all the talking. But on our next tour, my older sister Lisa had a sore throat and wasn't supposed to talk. I figured my younger sister Danielle would do all the talking. But Danielle said, "No, you do it." I couldn't believe it. I said, "You've got to be kidding."

Then I remembered that my pastor had said God wanted to use me, so I said I'd do it.

At our shows, we often invite people to become Christians. When that time came, I was nervous, but I trusted God and spoke from my heart. People started coming forward to put their faith in God.

It's the most awesome thing that ever happened to me, to see God using me like that! He's done it many times since.

And to think it all started because I went to church.

SO, WHaT NEXT?

Sometimes you might want to sleep in on a Sunday morning. Other times, it might seem like you're going through the motions. But church isn't just a side dish to the main course of your faith journey. It's a vital part of your walk with God.

1. Today's verse (Acts 2:42) is in a chapter describing the early church. It includes lots of reasons for us to be excited about going to church: the work of the Holy Spirit, inspired preaching, lively discussion, the Lord's Supper, prayer, fellowship, and even miracles. Read all of Acts 2 and get a great picture of the benefits of church.

2. Think of people at church who have played a role in your spiritual growth—your senior pastor, youth pastor, Sunday school teacher, small-group leader, etc. Write each of them a thank-you note this week.

3. Ask God not only to help you grow spiritually at church but to show you how you can serve there as well.

THINK ABOUT IT

If you attend church faithfully, you can probably relate to Andrea's story: When you miss church, you realize you've missed more than just three hours of sitting around in a building on a Sunday morning. You've missed solid teaching, good music, warm fellowship, opportunities to use your gifts, and a chance to worship your Creator with other people. When you miss church, you can feel it in your soul. Why? Because church feeds your soul.

Andrea Baca
OF OUT OF EDEN

Photo by Frank Ockenfels3

GiNny OWens

I Thought I Had to Be Perfect

WHEN I THINK about some of the songs I wrote when I was much younger, I have to laugh. I mean, they're just so silly. I'll even make fun of myself in concert by singing some of those songs today. I've learned that it's okay to laugh at myself.

I've also learned that it's okay to look silly in front of other people. I'm cool with that.

I haven't always felt this way. I used to take myself far too seriously. I used to believe that to earn the respect of others, I had to be a cut above the rest—that I had to be better than everyone else.

I used to think that way about God, too—that I had to excel in order to deserve his love. I had very little understanding of God's grace.

Then I started reading a book by Philip Yancey called *What's So Amazing About Grace?* I couldn't believe what I was discovering about God's grace. I had to learn more, so I began searching my Bible.

That search took me to Galatians 5:1, which begins, "So Christ has really set us free. Now make sure that you stay free . . . " It almost sounds redundant, using the word *free* back-to-back like that. But for stubborn people like me who just don't get it, repeating the concept isn't a bad idea.

Then I read the rest of the verse: " . . . and don't get tied up again in slavery to the law."

> So Christ has really set us free. Now make sure that you stay free, and don't get tied up again in slavery to the law.
>
> GALATIANS 5:1

That's when it hit me: I had been a slave to my own expectations. I didn't have to be perfect after all. God's grace—the fact that he loves me no matter how well or how badly I perform—gives me freedom.

It's not a freedom to mess around and do whatever, but it's a freedom to be the person God has created me to be. That's just been such a wonderful concept for me to embrace.

SO, WHAT NEXT?

Because God is perfect, even our very best efforts fall short of his standard. So we could never do enough to earn his acceptance. That's why we need Christ. As today's verse says, he brings us freedom—from having to work for God's love and approval.

1. Read Colossians 1:21-22. When Christ saves you, how does it change God's view of you? Read Ephesians 2:8-9. According to these verses, what role do you play in salvation? What does this say about God's love for you? How is this a freeing concept?

2. Take some time to explore the depths of God's grace. Start with the following verses: Luke 15:11-32, Romans 5:6-8, Colossians 2:13-15, 1 Timothy 1:15-16, Titus 3:4-7. You might also want to read the book Ginny mentioned, *What's So Amazing About Grace?* by Philip Yancey.

3. Thank God for loving you no matter how well—or how poorly—you perform. Ask him to help you believe this truth.

THINK ABOUT IT

Ginny once thought she had to excel in everything in order to be accepted by others. Not surprising. We're taught from a young age that success gets a pat on the back, while failure brings criticism. But Ginny learned that her value doesn't depend on performance. It only matters that through Christ she's a child of God. Do you believe that, or are you still trying to prove yourself to others—and to God?

Ginny Owens

Photo by Dorian Caster

Jaci Velasquez

Red, Yellow, Black, and White

I LOVE THE FACT THAT God made all of us so different. I never thought about it much as a kid because I grew up in a part of Texas where there were lots of different races and nationalities. I just took the diversity for granted.

But when my family moved to Nashville in my late teens, it was clear I wasn't in Texas anymore. Most people were white; many had never talked with a Hispanic person before. And they saw me as different.

That's okay. I like the idea of being different. I also like making friends with people of other races. Back in Texas, that was no big deal; it just happened. In Nashville, it's been harder to find friends from different ethnic backgrounds, but I've done it by being more open to the people God brings into my life. Now my two best friends are Danielle, who's black, and Heather, who's white.

One of the great things about these friendships is that they expand my view of the world. I like to see how others live, how they show love to their family, and how they worship God.

Heather, for instance, grew up in the South and is really loyal to her family's faith. She attends services on Sundays and Wednesdays and goes to at least one Bible study every week. That's part of her culture. For Danielle, praising God involves lots of singing, and she's very open about her faith. In my culture, faith is more personal, more private and intimate.

There is no longer Jew or Gentile, slave or free, male or female. For you are all Christians— you are one in Christ Jesus.

GALATIANS 3:28

Both of these friends have helped me become more excited and open about my beliefs. And I think my own intimate relationship with God has helped them see the importance of living out faith even when you aren't in church.

No matter how different we are, the important thing is that we are all striving for a better relationship with God. And ultimately, that's what holds us together and makes us such great friends.

THINK ABOUT IT

Jaci loves meeting people of different colors and cultures because it broadens her worldview and gives her an appreci-ation for God's cre-ativity and diversity. What about you? Do you have friends from different races? What have you learned from each other? Have there been any tensions because of your cul-tural or ethnic dif-ferences? How did you resolve them? What's the best thing about getting to know people of different races?

SO, WHaT NEXT?

Paul's letter to the Galatians isn't warm and mushy. He rips on them for practicing a type of racism—a racism that makes them cling so tightly to their Jewish customs that they come across as snobs. Galatian Jews who converted to Christianity looked down their noses at non-Jews who had become Christians, treating them as sec-ond-class citizens. And Paul called them on it.

1. Read Galatians 3:1-3. Why was Paul so angry? Now read 3:26-29. What else would you add to that list in verse 28? Black or white? Others? Read Ephesians 2:11-14. What does this passage say to you about ethnic and racial differences?

2. If you have a friend from another race, discuss these verses together. Then say, "Tell me something about your culture or your family history that I don't already know. Educate me." Then you do the same.

3. Ask God to give you more appreciation for ethnic and racial diversity. If you don't already have a friend from another race, ask God to give you more opportunities to interact with people from other cultures and backgrounds.

Jaci Velasquez

I Can't Wear That!

BEFORE MY SISTER Erica and I became known as Mary Mary, we sang backup vocals for different artists.

There was one guy I used to sing for, and I loved his music— good, wholesome stuff. But when we went out on a concert tour, things changed. The choreography was very sexual, and we had to wear these clothes that made us look like sex objects. I say "clothes" kind of loosely, because we really weren't wearing very much at all.

Tina Atkins of Mary Mary

> Don't you know that your body is the temple of the Holy Spirit, who lives in you and was given to you by God?
>
> 1 CORINTHIANS 6:19

I realized that what I was doing was wrong. God says my body is his temple, and he tells us to avoid doing stuff that could make others fall into sin. I knew that if I was onstage wearing what they wanted us to wear, moving the way they wanted us to move, it would certainly make guys in the audience think impure thoughts. So I had to quit singing with that group.

As a Christian, I'm supposed to represent Jesus to the world around me. But it's hard to do that if I'm wearing something skintight that shows every curve of my body. It's hard for me to talk about Jesus if I'm dressed like that. It sends out a confusing message, and it's just plain wrong.

It doesn't matter what my intentions are. Even if I'm not trying to be sexy, if I'm wearing skimpy clothes, some people— especially guys—can get the wrong idea. I'm not saying I should wear ankle-length dresses or anything drastic. I'm just saying I need to think about what others might think.

When I'm trying to decide what to wear, I always ask, *Would God approve of this?* Or maybe, *If somebody else was wearing this, what would I think of that person?*

People are always looking at us. If they don't know God, we might be the only chance they'll get to meet him. That's why we have to represent him well, not only in what we do and say but even in what we wear.

SO, WHaT NEXT?

Modesty means more than making sure you're properly covered. The amount of time you spend on your appearance is also a factor. There's nothing wrong with wanting to look nice, but when it begins to consume your thoughts and your time, a priority check is in order.

1. Read 1 Timothy 2:9-10 and 1 Peter 3:3-4. What would it look like to make yourself attractive by the good things you do? How would doing this contribute to inner beauty?

2. How much time do you spend working on your outward appearance? How does that compare to the amount of time you devote to inner beauty? Make a list of what you need to spend more or less time doing. Then start making changes.

3. Tell God you want to honor him with your body. Ask for his guidance in choosing the types of clothes you wear. Also ask him to help you focus more on inner beauty than outward appearance.

THINK ABOUT IT

According to fashion magazines and the clothes sold in popular stores, showing skin is in. Tina pointed out that buying into these styles can present problems for Christian girls. Why should you consider this when you make clothing choices? When it comes to what you wear, what does it mean to "honor God with your body" (1 Corinthians 6:20)?

Tina Atkins OF MARY MARY

Photo by Melinda DiMauro

TRicia BrOck
OF SUPERCHIC[k]

THE REAL SECRET TO POPULARITY

I CHANGED high schools my sophomore year, and it wasn't easy because I was pretty shy. I went from a small school that was practically like family to a much larger school, which made the move even harder.

How would I make new friends?

I wasn't too sure how that would happen, but I made a very big decision when I made that move: I wasn't going to sacrifice my standards to become popular. I wasn't going to worry about being in the in-crowd, going to the parties, and all that stuff. I just was not willing to do those things.

So many people put their confidence in whether they have a boyfriend, whether they're a cheerleader, whether they're invited to all the parties. But I just decided I wasn't going to play that game.

Instead, I made a choice just to try to love people and see what would happen. I decided to seek out people who were getting picked on and just try to be a friend.

There was this one girl whose self-esteem was low because people made fun of her, right to her face. She never had any friends, never had anyone to sit with. So I sat with her and became her friend.

I wrote her notes, sat with her, hung out with her. I later got a letter from her saying she had thought about suicide, but that she'd decided not to because of our friendship. If that was

Don't just pretend that you love others. Really love them. Hate what is wrong. Stand on the side of the good. Love each other with genuine affection, and take delight in honoring each other. . . . Don't try to act important, but enjoy the company of ordinary people.

ROMANS 12:9-10, 16

the only reason I went to that school, then I thank God for putting me there.

The funny thing is, I did end up being fairly popular at that school—not because I tried to be, but because I reached out and I cared about people. Which just goes to show that you don't have to sacrifice any of your standards or morals to be liked. People will respect you because you take the time to care.

THINK ABOUT IT

We all want to be affirmed and accepted by others, and there's nothing wrong with that. But the big question is, are we willing to do anything in order to be popular? Tricia decided popularity wasn't worth selling out on her standards, so she decided to go the unpopular route by paying attention to people who weren't necessarily cool. What about you? What are you willing to do—or not do—to become popular?

SO, WHaT NEXT?

What things have you done to make yourself more popular—or at least to look better in the eyes of others? Would Jesus have done the same thing?

1. Considering the size of the crowds that followed him around, Jesus was clearly very popular. But he never tried to befriend the "in-crowd"—namely, the powerful religious leaders of the day. Jesus often criticized those leaders (see Matthew 23:13-33) and instead turned his compassion to the outcasts, to the unpopular—healing them, forgiving them, encouraging them, hanging out with them. Read Luke 5:27-32. What can you learn from Jesus' example?

2. Jesus said healthy people don't need a doctor, but sick people do. Who in your life is spiritually "sick" and in need of a "doctor"? List five practical ways you can play that role, and commit to doing at least one of those things this week.

3. Ask God to give you the eyes of Jesus, to help you be more concerned with people than with popularity.

Tricia Brock

OF SUPERCHIC[K]